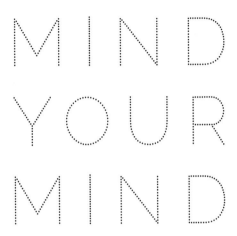

MIND YOUR MIND

using the power of words

BY AMANDA PEET

Cover image by: Copyrite
Book design by: SWATT Books Ltd

Printed in the United Kingdom
First Printing, 2021

ISBN: 978-1-8383644-0-3 (Paperback)
ISBN: 978-1-8383644-1-0 (eBook)

Amanda Peet Publishing
www.amandapeet.org.uk

Contents

PART TWO 69

Appendix 113

A note from the author

I have always had a love of words. My mum used to take me to the bookshop in Hebden Bridge, the nearest town to the village I grew up in. I was always in heaven – I dreamt of having the book showing all the Flower Fairies and I used to love looking at all the books.

What I would come away with was a *Spellwell* book: a small red and white stripy book (there was a series of them) that had lists of words in it.

That was it: just lists of words.

I remember the excitement of looking at it on the bus and then getting home and asking my poor mum, again and again, to test me on my spellings.

I loved learning new words. I loved that feeling of satisfaction when Mum read them out and I tried to spell them and got them right!! I loved **The Words** and even at that age, words were my passion.

Fast forward 42 years and I still love a list of words. What's changed now is that it's in the form of emotions and core beliefs. Knowing the transformation that those words can give you, gives me a buzz.

That's my passion, knowing that I am sharing words and that those reading those words may get the same excitement I do.

I know that if you do anything with the words you read in this book, by finding out why some stick, and working with *The Words*, then you are going to feel so much better.

My Mission: Shiny Happy People, so come and join me and shine!

Chapter 1

Introduction

Words are everywhere, they are all around us. We say them, we see them, write them, hear them and we keep them. The motto in our house is, 'Everything we say and everything we do, must be kind'.

Not all words are kind words. There are happy words, sad words, and nasty hurtful words. There are lovely, wonderful, encouraging words, which tell us, 'YES we can do it'. Whenever words are spoken there is a reaction, our reaction. When we read them, say them or hear them, we talk back, take action or withdraw action. We make decisions and we react… and that reaction depends on what life events you have experienced.

When I talk about 'life events' in this book, I am talking about anything that you have experienced that has brought a negative emotion to the surface. We can have good life events, and bad life events. Falling down the stairs is a life event, losing a loved one is a life event. Moving house is a life event where you might experience the good and the bad. Our life events are individual to us. Our reaction to those life events is individual to us. Even when we experience the same life event as someone else, there will be some similarities in our reaction when we talk to others about how we feel. We all react depending on what emotions and core beliefs we have in our subconscious minds, and no two are the same.

You can say the same words to ten different people and provoke ten different reactions. When we speak to each other, thoughts happen, actions happen, and emotions happen. We then experience a reaction to that emotion. It's ongoing, they don't stop. We don't stop experiencing and feeling emotions.

If an emotion remains in your 'system' from a life experience then that emotion feels strong, sometimes as strong as when you first experienced it. That can be 10, 20, or 30 years ago. Our emotions come and go and when we hold onto them, it's like having a little bank of them, a little account for each emotion that we just keep adding to. Because, somewhere along the way, it made sense to hang onto that emotion and not release it.

Words are all around us and so, consciously and subconsciously, we take them in. What you do with them then depends on your emotional health, emotional wellbeing and emotional knowledge. This book will explain what emotions and core beliefs are, what they can do, and how they behave. It will give you a greater understanding and, in turn, this can then help you to take charge of your mind to 'Mind Your Mind'.

Whoever you are, wherever you are from, whatever your background, whatever you have or haven't done, whatever you have or haven't got... we all have emotions and thoughts. If those thoughts persistently come into your mind, then you are not in your happy place! When your brain summons up a memory, it doesn't know the difference between then and now; it generates the same emotions as if it were happening now, all over again... unless you ask it not to.

Whatever your beliefs are in this world – religious, spiritual, law of attraction, universal energy, god, whatever it is – we are all human. Being human means having a cognitive brain, and that brain stores things. This storing helps us to remember the amazing things we have achieved throughout our lives and lets us share those experiences with others. Our brains also store the not-so-good stuff. It holds onto that feeling of being cross at that kid in the playground from when you were five. It holds onto why your brother and sisters were never in trouble and you were. It holds onto the heartbreak that other people have caused you. Your brain tells you to hold onto these so that you remember, and so that you don't ever let these things happen again... it holds onto life events.

What you keep stored in your brain depends on your life experiences.

What we will investigate in this book is how you can adopt, store, and release negative core beliefs and emotions.

What you choose in life and how you choose to react and behave in life, has a massive impact. 5% of our decisions come from our conscious mind. You might think you are consciously making all your decisions, but ooh nooo, 95% of your actions, decisions and choices are made because of the information stored and kept in your subconscious mind. This storage begins as soon as we exist.

In this book, we will look at what a core belief is. I will give you lists of core beliefs which you can read through for yourself. You can then decide, for each negative core belief, do I want to keep it or ditch it? I know what my answer is, to any limiting belief... off you go.

You may have heard of core beliefs and you may have heard people talking about limiting beliefs. Here is my interpretation:

Positive core beliefs are the statements that we hold to be true. Our principles, morals and integrity are of a positive nature, for example, **I am strong**, **I am kind**, **I am a good person**.

A negative core belief is something you have taken to be your truth from a life experience or that you have inherited and is in your subconscious. You may or may not know it is there. Often people will call it a limiting belief as that is what it does. It limits you.

A negative core belief limits the fullness to which you can experience your positive core beliefs. For example, **I am strong**, can be underpinned with **I am useless**, **I can't do this**, **I have to be strong**, or **I can't cope**. All of these are negative core beliefs and once recognised and cleared or released, they allow your positive core beliefs to be clear with no interference from negative limiting beliefs.

Positive and negative core beliefs are small sentences. Examples of negative core beliefs are:

> **I am not worthy**
> **I am useless**
> **I can't get anything right**
> **I can't trust anyone**
> **It's all my fault**

These small sentences, sometimes just 4 or 5 words, have so much power. Through life events and via other people, words have put them there, so what if… words can take them away??

Read on, my friend, and let us enter a world that is within all of us but sometimes so hidden we don't even know it is there…

It is amazing…

Whilst writing this book I re-read research from some years ago, as well as reading new books that I found fascinating, that support my work. I now know these books were the foundations and some of the building blocks to help me explore further what I needed to develop. I'm so proud of my 36-year-old self for picking up those books, for reading those articles, for listening to those interviews. I am proud of doing things that sound simple and easy for me now, but back then, I was dealing with depression, and every day felt like an age.

As I was finding the relevant snippets for this book, what I found truly amazing was how words of ours and words of others can become so interconnected over time and space.

In 1972, Candace Pert, Ph.D., based in the US, used words to conduct conversations with other scientists. Their words, mixed with her words and her extremely hard work, worked out, in October 1972, the science behind opiate receptors. For the purposes of this book I don't intend to go into what an opiate receptor is.

In turn, this science proved to be extremely important for the study of emotions and how the molecules of emotions work in the mind and the body.

One woman's determination and strength all those years ago, two years before I was born, has been so important all these years later in understanding the human brain and body. Without her work, and the work of many others, I wouldn't have my work. All these are pieces in a huge jigsaw of life. I find that amazing and I wanted to share that with you.

This book isn't all science – what I wanted to do was give you a brief overview and a brief history which takes us to where we are now in understanding that you can Mind your Mind, using the power of words.

In 1983, Candace Pert wondered, after doing some science,

"...perhaps this was an indication that communication was taking place not just within the brain, but between the brain and the rest of the body."
Candace Pert, Ph.D.,
Molecules of Emotion, page 127

What I love is that she was wondering, daydreaming, and thinking around her subject. When I heard that, "Words put it there, words can take it away", that set me off wondering and it's a wonderful feeling to wonder. Before I get into any more tongue twisters, what else I find interesting is that this science was breaking in 1983. That isn't that long ago; at the time of writing this it was 37 years ago. So, in terms of things developing, when people say, "Well, if things were that easy why haven't we always known this?", well this is why. Things develop.

I feel lucky enough to be alive at this specific time when all things mental health have dipped down to their very worst. This means that there is only one way to go: things can only get better. And if you are as old as I am, then you'll have an '90s song stuck in your head now, oops soz!!

What IS a long time ago is when 'Our Darwin' (I'm a Yorkshire lass, we have 'Our Mum', 'Our Mand'...) was alive, briefly:

Charles Robert **Darwin** FRS FRGS FLS FZS (12 February 1809 – 19 April 1882) was an English naturalist, geologist and biologist, best known for his contributions to the science of evolution.

Told you I'd be brief, thanks Wikipedia.

> *"Darwin himself could write only about the physiology of emotions and not about their biochemistry or genetics because the concept of biochemistry, with its specific components... would not be discovered for almost a hundred years."*
> Candace Pert, Ph.D.,
> *Molecules of Emotion*, page 134

Things take time, people take time to do things, and when those people have done things, other people can then do their things. If I had been born 50 years earlier, I wouldn't be doing the work I am doing now because time wasn't ready. Other people needed to do their things to become their part of the jigsaw.

Around the same time (1983), Candace Pert was experiencing this:

> *"I barely glimpsed it then, but the work we were doing in my lab during this time was laying the groundwork for a huge discovery, one that would lead us to formulate a radical theory that explained the link between mind and body, and how the emotions are directly involved with health and disease."*
> Candace Pert, Ph.D.,
> *Molecules of Emotion*, page 129

What Candace was working on is relevant to the way that we can use words today. Later in this book, we will look at how we can tell our subconscious what we want to happen.

Our brain is super clever, and we don't consciously use a massive part of it, the part that is running or ruining our lives, depending on how you look at it. We can do this, easy peasy lemon squeezy, as we will find out later.

Candace also writes...

> *"Most of our body/mind attentional shifts are subconscious... we are not consciously involved in deciding what gets processed, remembered and learned. But we do have the possibility of bringing some of these decisions into consciousness"*
> Candace Pert, Ph.D.,
> *Molecules of Emotion*, page 146

This is great news and is exactly what we will be doing later. We will be seeing what is in that subconscious mind, seeing what emotions and negative core beliefs are there, and then getting rid of them, changing them, changing your brain.

Words put these things there in the first place. Then, life experiences put these things there, things that have happened, things that are still producing an emotion or negative feeling within our bodies and minds.

So, thank you, Candace Pert. Thank you for doing your thing, so that many others can now do their thing.

The first half of this book is the 'Why' and the second part is the 'How'. Once you have read this fully, I hope this book will become a faithful handbook and companion for your emotional healthcare.

> "Knowledge is power and consequently, knowledge of self provides self-empowerment"
> Bruce Lipton, Ph.D.

PART ONE

Chapter 2
Mind Your Mind

Do this every day for the rest of your life, do this every morning when you get up, do this every night before you go to sleep.

Those have been some of the things I have read over time where my brain went "whhaaaatttt, no way", I want to live my life, not have to perform an endless routine of 'stuff' before I get going. I want my cup of tea with my morning thoughts, trying to remember what my dream was and why was I dreaming of Ant and Dec again, and then ease myself into what I have to do: make breakfast, do my work, play with Lego, make a den, pretend to be Maleficent or whatever other delights my 5-year-old daughter has in store for me.

I don't want a to-do list before I start my to-do list. Having said that, without all these instructions on how to start or end your day, I may not have been prompted to investigate just what you can do to sort the stuff out in your head. Also, I don't usually wake up leisurely; it's normally a little person donking me on the head with a toy at 5.30am – not my ideal way to come round after a great sleep. However, I do have things that I do each day or each week as part of my self-care but not to a strict routine. I undertake the self-care things that are right for me at that time.

When it comes to my emotional health, I want to be able to look after my mind, identify what it is upset about and sort it. That's it. Job done. Move on to the next thing.

Not everyone is comfortable with affirmations, afformations® (Noah St. John), mantras, or chants. Some people thrive on them but for many others, there is no alternative. What if you are not spiritual or religious, or what if you are religious and prayers just don't seem to have the right oomph to shift this stuff? This stuff is what we accumulate from life events.

Things happen to us, and before you have the chance to sort something out and process that life event, life throws you something else to deal with, which tips your jigsaw of life upside down.

Now what do you do with the pieces? It is exhausting having to start from the beginning and piece things back together every single time.

So, wouldn't it be great if you knew you could do something that, when the sh*t hits the fan again, prevents your jigsaw pieces of life being all tipped back into the box or thrown up into the air? Instead, there are a few pieces still intact, so you can say: "Aha, this has happened but look, I am here, and I still have this to build on... So, not this time Life. Oh no, my friend, we are getting back on track now, no longer will I be hiding under my duvet for 6 months... now Life, now I tell you, I can do this!"

Well, it is possible, read on...

Get to the root of things: isn't that what everyone knows they should be doing? Get to the heart of the issue, but what if that is too painful and feels impossible to navigate? Well, here is why it feels that way.

Our conscious mind works at 2,000 bits per second, and when you start to delve into it, or even when you just start to think about things that have happened, or you are triggered, something occurs in your brain. When you start to look at life events that have caused you hurt and pain, your conscious mind connects to your subconscious mind, which runs at 400 billion bits per second. For this reason, our subconscious throws all sorts of things forward, things that we didn't even know it had stored. These are things it has taken a snapshot of years earlier, before that 'life event'; and our poor conscious mind just can't keep up.

It is like have a super-fast computer running at 400 billion bits per second sending information to another computer that runs so slowly, like dial up. For those that don't remember dial up, it was sometimes quicker to walk! 400 billion bits per second sending to a computer running at 2,000 bits per second. Now, you can imagine the overload and error messages that will produce. That is what happens to our brain. Overload.

Our subconscious mind is so fast that it throws too much stuff forward. This causes our slower, conscious mind to start to shut down with overload. Or it sends you into a panic attack, or you just stop and think, I can't, I just can't go on.

At that point, here is what we do: many of us try too hard to consciously work everything out. This generates an emotion such as embarrassment. Here is an example we will all be familiar with:

A mum is out in a coffee shop with her young child. That child accidentally spills a drink, all over the table. The mum feels embarrassment and starts to try and sort it out. The child starts crying because in his little mind he is now in trouble. The crying makes the mum worse, and in amongst all of this the mum's subconscious – which by the way, being the subconscious mind, has no sense of humour, no concept of time, no manners or empathy – decides to bring to the front of her mind all those times in her life when she has ever been embarrassed.

Now, when you have something (your unconscious mind) as fast as 400 billion bits per second sending all that information to something (your conscious mind) that can process at only 2,000 bits per second, it's going to cause overwhelm, often feelings similar to a panic attack, where the heat just rises through your body. It is also going to bring on all sorts of other emotions that are linked to the embarrassment generated from the life events that have happened in the past.

In that moment, it is just a spilt drink. Looking from the outside, what should be a simple task to clean it up now becomes an overwhelm of emotions that you can't deal with. This is not because you are a rubbish mum, or haven't slept, or you are feeling judged by the whole world right now, but simply because your conscious brain isn't fast enough.

Our conscious mind works at 2,000 bits per second, so it is pretty busy, constantly processing everything we see, hear, taste, smell and remember. So, if you ask it to process anything in addition to this, it can't cope. That is, your body, your brain can't cope, not you, not you as a person, but your brain. It is how it works.

It would be like asking a child's pedal car to race alongside Formula One. The brain, that part of it, is just not fast enough.

We all beat ourselves up about not being able to do this or to do that, but what if we looked at it from a different angle? What if we said, OK, I've been using my brain this way and it just doesn't seem to be cutting it for me. What if you just needed to let a different part of your brain do the work it was made to do: the fast part that we rarely consciously connect to. What if our conscious mind decided to hand over the nitty-gritty and delegate it to the fast part, the part that has all of our memories, beliefs, emotions, and programming that we haven't consciously chosen to keep but we also haven't consciously chosen to clear out?

Well...

We need to bypass the conscious mind and go straight to the subconscious. We can then unravel, identify and ask to remove what is out of date, what is keeping us stuck. When that has been done, that same superfast part of your brain can take on all that processing, leaving our wonderfully chilled-out conscious mind to find the space for some quality thinking time. In the process, you are able to find clarity, without all the conscious mind graft... wonderful!!

Later we will be looking at how we can kick your negative core beliefs and emotions into touch and eliminate those that don't belong there. Move those out that have been squatting all this time!!

> "For there is nothing either good or bad, but thinking makes it so."
> William Shakespeare

Mind Your Body

Minding your Mind also helps you to look after your body. Words create a neurological and biological response in your mind *and* your body. What happens in your mind has a direct impact and consequences in your body.

> "Biological behaviour can be controlled by invisible forces, including thought."
> Bruce Lipton Ph.D.,
> The Biology of Belief, page 84

I have had many clients over the years who have come to me with physical pains, but by clearing emotions and stuck limiting beliefs, I have had pain-free clients walking out of their session.

Dr David Hamilton puts it nicely:

> *"Many people, if they have been sick for a long time, affirm their conditions with statements like, 'This is terrible', 'I'll never get better', and 'I feel tired.' While these statements are accurate reflections about how they feel, they also back up the condition on a biological level, as neurons are stimulated in the appropriate areas of the brain, chemicals are released, and genes are switched on and off. So, the cells linked with the disease are encouraged to produce proteins and other substances that sustain the diseased state."*
>
> Dr David Hamilton,
> *How Your Mind Can Heal Your Body*, page 108

With negative core beliefs relating to illness, it is not a case of forcing yourself to feel better and trying to 'think positive'. When you identify and release/clear a negative core belief, you start to think more positively, naturally. And your body responds to that.

If you are ill, have a disease or are in pain, then common negative core beliefs, limiting reactions, or limiting justifications to yourself, are listed here, some of which you may recognize as your own or what you have heard other people say. The more core belief work you do, the more you will see and hear them springing up all over the place:

I will never get better
I have to live with this
I have to manage this illness
This won't ever go away
This belongs to me
I have to have this illness
Other people are worse than me

The last one is an underpinning ringleader for many and can form the basis for other issues. Yes, there will be people that are in a worse position health-wise than you but that is no reason for you to be unhealthy and in pain. Feeling that *other people are worse than me* gives you permission to hold onto your illness, disease or pain. You start to feel that you do not deserve to get better while others are so much more ill than you. When your system has hung onto this negative core belief you are unknowingly taking ownership for how ill you are. When you take ownership of an illness it can start to become part of your identity and who you are. The illness is yours and the more you hold onto it the more it keeps you stuck where you are. You are unable to allow the illness to pass through your system as you keep it and own it.

The following is interesting:

> *"Two people can have an identical illness, but one may suffer much more than another. The difference is in each person's attitude."*
> Dr David Hamilton,
> *How Your Mind Can Heal Your Body*, page 158

And I will tell you why. A positive attitude has been proven in many scientific studies to help you to improve your health. If your positive core beliefs are in line and in agreement with a positive attitude, then you don't need to use up precious energy forcing yourself to have a positive attitude. You don't need to wear a positive-attitude mask. I have heard people saying, *"I will make myself happy"*. Well, sadly, that isn't possible, you can't just "make" yourself happy. All that can ever be is a temporary mask. You need to clear something out, change things, and then being happy has a chance of occurring naturally. Further than that, permanently discarding negative core beliefs gives more room for positive core beliefs to become permanent and sustainable for that natural, unforced, feeling of happiness. Does that make sense?

Your brain can be wired to agree that:

I *can* be happy
I *can* be healthy
This *will* pass
I *am* allowed to be healthy
I *love* my body
My body and mind *are* amazing
I *will* look after myself
My body and mind *are* getting stronger and healthier

If that happens, your superfast subconscious is wired up to agree with your positive (conscious mind) attitude, and it starts to communicate this to your body. Cells begin to change in accordance with your beliefs and your body starts to feel different.

When your conscious and subconscious agree, in a good way, that's when Minding Your Mind and Minding Your Body start to work in sync with each other, with amazing results.

What about these little nuggets that can stay rent-free in your subconscious for years!!

I am not enough
I am useless
I can't do anything
I am not worthy
I am worthless
I am useless

> "A lack of self-worth can be an underlying cause of some illnesses."
> Dr David Hamilton,
> *How Your Mind Can Heal Your Body*, page 161

Identifying and changing your negative core beliefs helps to increase your sense of self-worth, self-esteem, confidence, and helps you to see how you can take responsibility for yourself in a much more positive and empowered way.

Taking responsibility

From the moment we are born we are responsible for ourselves. Babies choose to feed or not feed, sleep or not sleep, cry or not cry, depending on the reactions from grown-ups around them to these choices. They then make decisions based on what they know, plus the influence of this added information from grown-ups.

We take responsibility for ourselves in all sorts of ways and then behave accordingly, based on what we observe, hear, and learn. We make decisions for ourselves: what we drink, when we cross the road, what time we go to bed, what we say, and how we behave.

There may be times in your life when you have heard yourself saying, *"It's their fault, it's because of what they did"*. It may be that this is something that is part of your life at the moment. We all react like this, at some point. We do this to shift responsibility away from us or at least to try to shift it.

Are any of these statements familiar, either as thoughts you have had, or as things you have heard others say:

I behave like this because they did this to me
I can't be nice, because this happened to me
I will never be happy, because they did this to me
It's their fault
I can't ever forgive them
They have ruined my life

Notice anything? They are also all limiting beliefs. Limiting beliefs that are borne out of a specific life experience or event. There are many events, experiences or moments in time that can make you feel this way. As well as being beliefs, they can also be statements, often all too true statements. Maybe they did ruin your life at that time, and because the emotions from that experience are still with you, you have relinquished responsibility, or feel that responsibility for your life has been taken away from you. The good news is that you can take back responsibility for your life, and the fact that you are reading this means you are already taking steps to do that.

It is possible to free yourself from life experiences that made you feel a certain way, because that was then, and this is now. The chapters in the second half of this book show you the HOW, once you have learned the WHY.

I have worked with many people in their 30s, 40s, 50s, right up to their 80s, and they have all been running on some old limiting beliefs from when they were a child. You wouldn't let a child make important decisions for you, or probably any decisions on your behalf, yet here we are letting our own childhood beliefs run the show. Your show, your life.

The earlier you can get to grips with this the better.

You won't have wasted time, but you may have chosen to do different things with your time if you weren't in a constant battle letting your child within lead the way. The good news is that you can start to make changes at any age. The exciting thing is that you can do this yourself and you can get started as soon as you are ready to give it a go.

There is nothing stopping you, only yourself. If you are unsure where to start, identify one of your limiting beliefs and discard it. See how that feels, leave it a week, then try another. Once you have released a limiting belief, it has gone. I will be teaching you the HOW, but for now, I want you to understand the WHY.

A common limiting belief from childhood, for those of us with siblings, is:

I am not important

Well, why would you be? You had Mum and Dad all to yourself, looking at you, laughing with you, having fun, playing, answering your every question. And then: 'They' came along, that baby brother or sister who then made sure that you got no Mummy and Daddy time for yourself. This is a common limiting belief for those with siblings, and not just for the eldest.

There are so many ways that this belief can limit you. You habitually put yourself last; you fail to look after your health; you are susceptible to addictions and an unhealthy lifestyle; relationships all too easily become toxic; the list goes on… all because you have been holding onto this misguided belief. Every one of us *is* important, but these layers of behaviour make people lose sight of this.

This limiting belief can be reinforced for all sorts of other reasons too. This includes children whose parents are separated and one or both parents take up with a new partner. The child then may feel pushed out and not included. Not always, but this can happen all too often when the grown-ups are not fully considering how their actions are affecting the children around them.

Therapy v Do it Yourself

Most therapies start with you explaining what has happened. For example, you might get asked by a therapist, "What were your life experiences up to this point?"

The techniques in this book are designed to offer a way to bypass this talking phase and move straight to your mind's hard drive, to see what is limiting you from being free of your attachment to life events in the past.

This book is here to explain more about how to deal with emotions related to limiting beliefs. We will explore what they are, how we adopt them and store them, and why some feel so embedded we believe they will never leave us. When beliefs of this type have been with us for such a long time, they can feel like they have always been a part of us.

For anyone who is trying to process particularly significant life events, it is always my advice to seek out a qualified practitioner who can help you to explore and analyse those things that you may be blocking out rather than coming to terms with.

There is a great deal you can do yourself. But if you reach the limit of what you can do, then I do recommend that you ask for help from a professional. On my website, www.amandapeet.org.uk I have a list of practitioners who specialise in clearing limiting beliefs and emotions.

It's not a question of making a decision to choose between one or the other – a combination of self-care and professional help is always a good balance.

Self-Talk

We often tell ourselves off – it's a habit acquired in childhood. When we were young we were told off by those who loved us and guided us. Sometimes, later in life, we continue to hear those voices of parents, grandparents, grown-ups at that time, and teachers. Those voices swirl around our head, still reminding us we are not good enough. But what if they were wrong? What if they got it wrong?

We have decided for ourselves what we should continue to hang on to, but what if we are wrong? What if we have decided to hold onto and take notice of something that wasn't true in the first place. We are now following an untruth. What if, as a child, you misunderstood? Isn't that more than likely?

Children hear half a conversation, earwig on what grown-ups are saying, pick up half a story and fill in the missing bits themselves. We have then acquired a limiting belief based on what, at best, was the snatch of something overheard as a child. Not exactly the most solid basis on which to live parts of your life. And once implanted and believed at such an early age, this has, over time, become a stuck negative core belief.

So why do we continue to tell ourselves off as a grown-up? It is in our programming.

How we talk to ourselves is important, and you have probably read this time and time again, but it's true: we need to be our own best friend. Talk to yourself how you would talk to others that you love and care about.

If you have negative core beliefs cropping up telling you that you are not worthy or useless or whatever the negative core belief may be, hear whose voice is saying that to you. It is likely not to be your own. We don't want to be talking to ourselves like a naughty 5-year-old. Be your own best friend.

> *"It is only by delving into the subconscious mind that you will be able to see how the belief system that you are operating with gives you information to act and respond in the world."*
> Sam Thorpe,
> *META Messages from Your Body*, page 186

Here are some examples of some limiting beliefs we may have convinced ourselves to be true:

I am a bad person
I am a bad mother
I am a bad father
I am a bad sister
I am a bad brother
I can't do anything
I can't fix this

The list goes on and on. What is interesting is that once we have made such statements and repeated to ourselves that limiting belief, we are then constantly looking for evidence to back it up. These false beliefs start to weigh heavily, and you then add more and more reasons to confirm them. Your brain says, "See, yes **it must be true** because..."

The next chapter looks at limiting beliefs and emotions in more detail and examines where they come from.

Chapter 3

Emotions and Core Beliefs... what are they?

Emotions

Emotions are something that we all experience, every day in one way or another. Here are two that you will be familiar with:

Happy
Sad

Probably one of the most basic questions we ask is: does this make me happy or sad? Happy and Sad are the overall emotions. Happy seems to cover all the positive emotions and Sad covers all the negative. In this book, we are going to delve into what other emotions there are that come under Happy or Sad, positive or negative. The list in the second half of the book lists over 80 emotions... and that isn't all of them!

With Happy emotions, we like to hang onto them, but they don't always stay around. For example, can you remember being so excited about something that you thought you might pop? Maybe it was the anticipation of Christmas or opening your birthday present and that realisation as you opened it that it was exactly what you wanted. I get very excited in the run-up to a meal out, especially a Sunday roast dinner... yum!

You feel so good, sooooo happy and excited – jump up and down giddy excited. You are feeling in that moment all these wonderful emotions. That is a great life experience.

Within an hour you are not in the same height of excitement: you can recall the excitement, but you don't stay in that emotion. It has passed through for that life event. We all seem pretty good at that, allowing the positive emotions to come, be with us, and leave.

We know that we can feel that emotion again at another time in the future. If we all hung onto those emotions, we would all be going round in a state of excitement, on such a high that we wouldn't get anything done. Whilst you are in the height of the emotion it is difficult to concentrate on anything except that emotion.

With Sad emotions, the negative stuff, we should be able to treat these in the same way. For example, a pet passes away, and you feel loss, grief and all the other emotions that are linked to that pet.

Your grief could include guilt, shame and a whole range of other emotions. We feel emotions in the moment, and it can be the following day, week, months, and sometimes years later when we recall that memory. There they are: the emotions as raw as the day it happened.

It isn't as natural for the sad emotions to come, be with us, and leave in the same way the happy emotions do. This is to do with our wiring. How we have wired ourselves to deal with emotions, how we were taught to deal with emotions. Many will say, "My parents didn't explain to me how to deal with emotions". Many will know that they learned how not to do things from observing how their parents did things, making a vow such as: **"I will never do that to my kids."** We will be talking about vows in a later chapter.

Between the ages of 0-6 is the time when we all experience emotions for the first time. These are the years when our brains store information on how to deal with those emotions, based on what those grown-ups who are influencing us during those years are saying and doing when we are experiencing an emotion for the first time.

Dr. Lipton says:

> *"Young children carefully observe their environment and download the worldly wisdom offered by parents directly into their subconscious memory. As a result, their parents' behaviour and beliefs become their own."*
> Bruce Lipton Ph.D.,
> *The Biology of Belief,* page 163

So when you say, *"I refuse to be like my mother, grandparent, or carer"*, you can refuse all you like with your conscious mind, but when your subconscious contains their beliefs and behaviours, you have to change your mind, literally. This will take you nearer to being you rather than them.

> *"The fundamental behaviours, beliefs and attitudes we observe in our parents become 'hard-wired' as synaptic pathways in our subconscious minds. Once programmed into the subconscious mind, they control our biology for the rest of our lives... unless we can figure out a way to reprogram them."*
> Bruce Lipton Ph.D.,
> *The Biology of Belief,* page 164

Think of your subconscious mind as your hard drive, the place where everything is stored. Words put emotions and core beliefs there, so words can take them away. I would just like to point out that there are many good emotions and positive core beliefs in there too which we will keep. Surely, if it was that easy, then everyone would be doing this? Well, it depends on what their emotions and negative core beliefs are and how willing they are to change them.

As humans and in our families, we are conditioned to believe that it is difficult, it is hard work, it is even impossible to be mentally well. And yet those same people who are affected by many limiting beliefs would say they do not have mental health issues. Sounds to me like there is a core belief out of balance. We will come onto that later.

Our emotions also buddy up with each other. For example, when we experience grief at a moment of loss, it is common to experience shame and guilt during that grieving process. Your brain can think that it is a bad thing to process your grief and that you should carry it around with you always, like an internal sign and reminder.

You are not going to forget that person when you are grieving. What you will do is remember, with love, all the days that person lived, without being stuck in the one day that they passed away.

As an example, I am going to share two stories about the same emotions and 'life event'.

Can you spot the difference and possible long-term effects?

Child one: A child is riding his bike and his dad is teaching him. The child comes off and, in that moment, he experiences shock, embarrassment, frustration, hurt and sadness. He has also grazed his knee, just a little. The child starts to cry... a lot! The dad, in a raised voice, says, "Stop crying, you're not hurt, get back on."

Child two: A child is riding his bike and his dad is teaching him. The child comes off and, in that moment, he experiences shock, embarrassment, frustration, hurt and sadness. He has also grazed his knee, just a little. The child starts to cry... a lot! The dad says, "Wow, that must be a shock. You were on your bike and then really quickly you ended up on the floor – that happens when you're learning. Are you crying because you are hurt? Look, there's a little graze but it's not bleeding. We will carry on when you're ready, here's a tissue."

Can you see the difference?

Child one: the child will experience those same emotions again, many times through his life, and his response to shock, embarrassment, frustration, hurt and sadness will be to hold it in and **get on with it**. The lasting effects of how to deal with emotions can carry on into our adult lives. Don't express emotions and hold them in, are damaging strategies to learn for our emotional health.

As a practitioner, many adults that I have seen are still dealing with emotions in the same way that they did when they were 4 or 5. When you get to 40 or 50 years old that is a lot of emotions, stuck, not processed in your system.

Child two: the child will experience those same emotions again, many times through his life but *his* response to shock, embarrassment, frustration, hurt and sadness will be to allow it, and acknowledgement that it is OK to feel those feelings.

He will also be able to work out and process what happened, as his dad described what the child didn't see, but felt. As a grown-up, this child is likely to be able to understand a situation, a life event, take stock of it, work out what has happened, process emotions, and let them go.

This is a broad example, to show you how support and reaction to emotions do matter. We of course don't know what the dad with child one was going through himself and how well he had been taught to deal with his emotions.

Men, especially, are told by society that it is not manly to be emotional. What *is* manly is to know how to deal with a piece of your body, your brain (men get told they have two brains and that they think with only one, but I don't believe that... not all of them anyway!! Wink, wink). If a grown-up doesn't know how to deal with emotions, what chance have their children got? It becomes the same pattern over and over, taught down family lines.

Men also have a resilience to hold trauma for longer then women. It is not a weakness, it's a difference in how males and females are wired. Men... choose to let it go chaps and feel your freedom without having to carry any trauma around with you. You will look and feel better.

There are many ways in which a child will react and how they will respond to falling off a bike, depending on what else is going on in their lives. However, as an example, this shows how emotional support from the grown-ups around us at this crucial age of 0-6 helps us to shape how we deal with emotions as an adult.

Now we are starting to understand what emotions and core beliefs are, so that you can understand a little of the neuroscience behind how **The Words** work. You have been learning the importance of knowing how you can reprogram your subconscious mind.

It is important to me, when developing these techniques, that this is something that you can undertake for yourself. This means that you can take responsibility for your subconscious mind, and you can clear it out. Just like you take responsibility for your body by cleaning your face, hands and teeth, and conduct body care and hair care as part of your self-care.

What if it could take just seconds to clear your limiting beliefs? Imagine things popping into your head and you are able to deal with them just as quickly as you would deal with washing your hands or wiping your face after eating messy ice cream (or is it just me that gets messy?!)

A few years ago, I was walking home one day, thinking about my business and how I was going to use Facebook, and I just thought, oh no, *I hate Facebook*. Aha, there's one, a negative core belief right there. Straightaway I knew why I hated it. Nevertheless, by the time I had got home ten minutes later, that negative core belief was no longer there. That's how easy it is when you know what to do. People walking past or driving past had no idea I was clearing out a negative core belief. I might have looked like I was talking to myself, but if I had been worried about that I would have just put my phone to my ear to look like I was on the phone.

In my experience, when you find a negative core belief, it moves fast and needs to be pinned down. Either write it down or deal with it there and then, because half an hour later you will be thinking about other things and you won't be able to recall it.

Think about all the times you have heard, or maybe you have said to a child, things that you meant as a throwaway comment:

- When a child is trying to solve a puzzle and is getting stuck, if you say, "Give it here, **you are useless**", that belief can become theirs. It doesn't need to be said over and over for a child to take ownership of it and believe those words from a grown-up.

- When a child is trying to tie their shoelaces at an age far too early for the child's ability, and the grown-up says, **"You can't do that"**. That can become stuck, and from that point it may take them much longer to learn to tie their shoelaces. The effect spreads wider than that, as those *I can't* beliefs can start to affect other activities and areas of life. So, the child begins to believe that they can't do other things that require a similar amount of thinking and working out. When they start to do something and they are reminded of trying to do their shoelaces, their subconscious will kick in with, *you can't*, reminding them that they can't.

- When a child is upset and crying, and you continually tell them to stop crying, when they feel like they want to cry in the future they may be reminded of this and so not cry. Their grown-ups' response has taught them to keep their feelings held in. Sounds familiar? I think that many grown-ups today feel like they have to keep their emotions in, especially males. Clearly, this is not a healthy option, but it is yet another consequence of what we do. Why? Because that is what has been passed down the ages.

When children hit that amazing time of puberty!!

Their brains are full of all the good stuff and the bad stuff that their grown-ups have helped to plant. No wonder this is a difficult age: bodies changing, stuff growing, hormones flying around, exams looming, and a subconscious that is programmed to tell them things that are not true for them. That is pretty rough going. I have always said that I would not want to relive my teenage years, which I found a complete struggle, but I *would* be tempted if I had the tools I have now and, from an experimental point of view, I would be fascinated to see what I could achieve.

Remember that feeling of being gutted when, as a teenager, you heard something that made you feel that you were worthless or that you couldn't do anything? Those emotions can stay with you and store themselves up so that the next time you feel the same emotions for a different reason, a different life event, your subconscious acts a bit like Google and says, "Here, have this lot too." 'This lot' are all the stored emotions that you haven't been able to get rid of, that match what you're feeling now.

If you don't want your subconscious to play 'Matchy Matchy' with all the emotions that you have stored up, it might be time to consider letting them go.

Your subconscious mind also doesn't have any empathy; it doesn't have a sense of humour, and it will do as it is told. It won't think, *'Oh, she's had a bad night's sleep, I won't do my job today'* or *'He's had enough to deal with this week'*. Your subconscious will just do its job, excellently, and in turn your conscious mind needs to deal with those consequences.

You can't just say, "I am going to think positively so that I don't let those emotions into my head, because I always turn to positive thoughts before they arrive". That is bloody exhausting. You can think positively, but if you think that is going to stop you from feeling stuck emotions, you are mistaken. Those emotions are still there, in your subconscious, so when you block them in this way, they find a way to be dealt with. It also uses an immense amount of energy to deal with emotions in this way. And you are consciously trying to think positively, which uses up energy in itself. When stuck emotions and negative core beliefs are released, there is no need to actively have to think positive, as you simply don't have the negative stuff there. As a result, you make choices and decisions from a much better place: a calmer, less cluttered place.

When emotions are not allowed to be processed and released, when your mind doesn't or can't deal with them, then your body lends a hand. A great deal of research has been done in this area, providing evidence that stuck emotions can manifest themselves as illnesses in your body.

Hold on or let go?

Many of us believe that we need to have a little of each negative emotion within us to be able to operate efficiently as human beings. You don't. Emotions come and go, that is their job. They are there to alert us to something in life that may or may not be 'up our street'. Holding onto emotions, though, especially negative emotions, can limit you.

If you were to let go of an emotion linked to a memory of a life event that happened in the past, that memory would still be there but the emotion you felt at the time will have gone. It came, it did its job, so let it be free. You will still feel that emotion again for another experience, but it won't feel as strong and you will know the cause, the root. By holding onto old emotions, it only increases the intensity the next time you feel it.

The mum in the coffee shop, if she releases all those emotions that she was holding onto the next time her child spills a drink, she will deal with it for what it is, a spilt drink. It won't give her a surge of emotions, because those emotions will hold no charge in her system.

Letting go of stuck emotions from old memories doesn't mean that you stop feeling emotions. You will always feel emotions. It is just that when you start releasing the old stuff, some of which is not even yours, but family stuff, the intensity isn't there. I have been looking after my emotions and core beliefs for over 12 years and if something makes me cross, I can get shouty and angry and say my piece. Then it is done. I am not more cross; I am cross just for that moment and that life event. I also check in with myself as to why I reacted like that, and generally find a negative core belief, so I get rid of that too. Better out than in.

Sam Thorpe explains this, from research:

> "We humans, unlike animals in the wild, do not release
> our shocks and traumas so easily. Instead, we tend to
> re-live unresolved situations in a continued attempt
> to resolve them. We fixate upon and go over our past
> experiences and we worry and fret about the future. This
> is because information from a traumatic event stays
> trapped, frozen in our energy and awaiting an opportunity
> for resolution. This accumulation of small and large
> traumas stored in the system is exhibited as stress. To
> compensate, the body continues to adapt in an attempt
> to assist us to protect ourselves against the ongoing and
> unresolved threat, until the danger has passed, and the
> issue is resolved. Then the body will enter into repair."
>
> Sam Thorpe,
> *META Messages from Your Body*, page 26.27

That last line is crucial to our understanding of just how much emotions and core beliefs affect us and our bodies. Our heads are attached to our bodies but how much do we really remember that? Let's say, you want to make a cup of tea. Before you know it, your legs have walked you to the kitchen and your hands are getting cups out. You might fill the kettle and flick it on, and only stop to consciously choose the cup to use (I have my favourites – the big ones for a lovely big cuppa). You had the thought and your body reacted.

Your head is definitely attached to your body: give your neck a wiggle, it really is. Your thoughts affect the whole of you. When you are affected by an illness such as depression, or aches and pains, you can take all the prescription drugs you want, they mask the root. Once the root, the emotion or negative core belief that is keeping you stuck is released, like Sam says above, "Then the body will enter into repair".

Why, then, do we always try to do it the other way around? Why do we try to get our bodies healthy and happy first when we should start with our minds? Minding your Mind can have amazing results on your health and wellbeing, and the good news is that it isn't hard work, it is really easy. Why shouldn't it be easy? Words put it there, so words can take it away.

In the introduction, I wrote about the time and space thing, you know... it was only 37 years ago that scientists could prove that our minds and bodies are connected so, of course, we couldn't have always done this. A car couldn't be made until an engine had been designed. *Our* engine has been around in the same design for years, but we are only, in recent years, getting the technology and information to see how it works.

At this point in writing, I am getting excited that you, whoever you are, reading this, will be able to do something that can instantly help you. Simply with words.

Core beliefs

These are small statements, powerful small sets of words that, once we take them on board, can lead us down a whole different path.

Some common negative core beliefs are:

I am useless
I don't trust anyone
I have to do it myself
I don't deserve
I am hopeless
I can't do anything
Everything I try goes wrong
I am never seen
I am never heard

Wherever I am I don't like it

These are all stored in our subconscious mind. Very few of us know that these are there or how they got there. Maybe it was something someone said to you or did to you and your brain decided to keep it. They are beliefs that we believe to be true about ourselves. Life events that have happened to us, around us or outside of us.

Let's take the example of a child trying to complete a jigsaw and they just can't find that one piece they are searching for. They give up, get cross and say, *"I can't do jigsaws"*. This can change and broaden into *I can't do puzzles. I can't work things out, I can't.* There it is: a negative core belief that is now in your subconscious and will limit you.

Years later, you can't quite work out why you find some aspects of work difficult, you are puzzled why you don't seem able to work some things out. You have a session with a professional, who tracks it back to a negative core belief that *I can't do jigsaws*. You release that, along with an amazing amount of anger that has built up over the years linked to that negative core belief. Hey presto, suddenly the work issues click into place and you 'get it'. You are no longer limited by an old outdated negative core belief.

Negative core beliefs can become stuck in your subconscious mind because you said it or did it, or someone said it or did it to you. Maybe you observed an event that made you think a certain way.

If not checked in on, these negative core beliefs can be stored, and then you act on them, as they are now part of your brain's programming. However, when a life event is over and that 'moment' has passed, the negative core beliefs can quickly become outdated.

A negative core belief of **I don't deserve** can come from all sorts of conversations, comments from our grown-ups, or from what we tell ourselves because of things that have happened. **I don't deserve** is the broad negative core belief. It might be that this started with:

I don't deserve nice toys
I don't deserve to have sweets
I don't deserve to be happy
I don't deserve presents from Father Christmas
I am bad
I am naughty

Negative core beliefs develop. What starts with **I can't cook** can turn into **I can't** across all areas of life. This can affect your relationships, work, family and friends, because the **I can't** bit has taken root.

Where do core beliefs come from?

What got me started on this route of wanting to find out more about core beliefs was simply a statement I read, around 2009, which was:

"If words put it there, words can take it away"

I have no idea what I was reading at the time, but this got me thinking, and I hear myself saying this often. The emotion or the negative core belief has arrived because of what one person has said to another person. While I find that this is a primary way in which these are implanted, there are many other ways in which we can take on a negative core belief. These include:

People
Life events
Inherited patterns

Reactions to an outside experience
Depression

Let's explore each of these a bit further:

People

They tell us stuff; they behave in a certain way and they do or say things to other people that then make those other people question and doubt themselves.

When a person is told repeatedly that they are useless, then that can stick. In the same way, sometimes a person only needs to be told once that they are useless and that can also stick. Parents, teachers, carers, friends, family, anyone you interact with, can say something that creates a negative core belief which stays with you and becomes your default. Many don't mean to; they don't even know they have done that. And yet each and every one of us has the ability to keep negative core beliefs, and unwittingly say something that causes another person to receive and keep one.

Phrases that you say, or that are common within your family, such as **money doesn't grow on trees** or **it runs in our family**, can be translated into negative core beliefs within your system. You hear them and say them so much that they become your truth.

As children and as adults, we all see, hear and learn all sorts of things and don't question that they might be a load of rubbish or a distorted version of the truth. Many untruths are just things that grown-ups were told as a truth and so they repeat them, unaware they are repeating things that are not factually correct.

What a child sees and hears has a huge impact on their behaviour as they grow up. Many say that a child who grows up with violence becomes violent. This is sometimes the case, but not always. Sometimes a child who grows up with unkind behaviours in their home sees how not to behave and chooses a different way to be. However, the things which that child has seen still leave a 'snapshot' which can come out as illness or can trigger other things like allergies, limiting behaviours, or depression in later life. The good news is that all this can be changed. We can change our thought patterns, and by the end of this book you'll be able to change yours. Liberating!!

As a child, perception can be highly confusing. How a child perceives the world is also linked to how they deal with the world. As we continue to grow into adults, we start to gain more and more information about the world around us and how, as an adult, we have different responsibilities. We have no way of knowing if a child has understood things in the way they were intended, as we have no way of knowing what their perception has been. It is important to show children things from different angles so that they are given a good chance of understanding things the way they were intended. The way they perceive and understand things comes from their world view and the information and knowledge that they currently have. It is all too easy to say things and expect children to understand what we are saying, in the way we do as adults.

I will give you an example. I asked my 5-year-old if she wanted to start learning Spanish. She said, yes, she would love to, and so she started. After the second lesson, we were sat chatting and she said, "Mummy, I don't think I want to learn Spanish anymore", and so I asked why that was. She said, "Mummy, if I speak Spanish then no one will understand me because my friends all speak English." Priceless!! I had to explain the whole thing around English being her first language and that Spanish would be her second language, to speak to her friends who can speak Spanish. In her mind, she thought she was learning Spanish to speak Spanish all the time and was worried that no one was going to understand her. From a 5-year-old's view, this makes perfect sense. It was her perception. After a chat about it, and her saying "Oh" quite a lot, she decided that she will continue to learn Spanish and isn't worried about it anymore.

Easy to see why things get so confusing if you haven't got grown-ups who are explaining things to you in a way that you can understand. Who knows what that could have turned into if it hadn't been worked out... possibly *I can't learn another language* or *nobody understands me*. The important thing to remember is that when you have a negative core belief, it is not always from a trauma. It can be from a simple misunderstanding, a misinterpretation or confusion that hasn't been discussed. It's good to talk, for so many reasons, especially to our children.

Life events

Things happen to us all the time which we refer to as life events. These can be births, deaths, marriages, relationships (the build-up and breakdown of), accidents, illness, moving house, new jobs, redundancy, exams, starting school, leaving school. The list is endless.

We keep negative and positive core beliefs from these significant moments, because at the time they were true. However, there comes a time after a life event when you need to question if you still need those core beliefs, negative ones in particular.

Life events can come in all shapes and sizes, and how your emotions have been guided as you were growing up depends on how you deal with them and also how you perceive them. The biggest trauma that has ever happened to you could be falling down the stairs. The biggest trauma for another person may be being witness to a murder. Both are different in terms of extreme, but if it is the worst thing that has ever happened to you it can leave a lasting impact, no matter what others' perceptions are.

As a therapist, when I was dealing with clients, I was never surprised to find out what was underneath the stuck emotions. Every client was treated the same no matter what my perception of the trauma was.

So, when you hear people saying, "Oh, that's nothing... such and such far worse happened to my friend", the person explaining their trauma can be made to feel that they shouldn't talk about theirs and so buries it, when in fact they should be allowed the time and space to talk about it, if that is what they want to do, and release what is stuck. Buried trauma weighs very heavily. Nobody should be carrying around emotions and negative core beliefs linked to their traumas.

Wherever negative core beliefs come from they have a huge impact on our mental, emotional and physical health.

"Now we know for certain – fact – that thoughts, emotions and beliefs are not just subjective ideas in the mind but cause real chemical and physical changes in the brain and throughout the body."
Dr. David Hamilton,
How Your Mind Can Heal Your Body, page xii

Scientific studies show how our mind affects our body, including our actions and illnesses. One study conducted by scientists at Yale University is rounded up nicely here by Dr. David Hamilton:

"And just as attitude affects the heart, the Yale scientists even concluded that attitude was more influential than blood pressure, cholesterol levels, smoking, body weight and exercise levels in how long a person lived."
Dr. David Hamilton,
How Your Mind Can Heal Your Body, page xii

By changing your mind, by changing the default settings that are currently there, you can change your physical health and your mental health, and in turn you can start to tackle those things like body weight and smoking, if you want to.

I have conducted work with smokers in the past, and during the sessions we didn't even talk about smoking. We just identified negative core beliefs that felt true to that person and then cleared them. The result was not wanting to smoke or not wanting to smoke as much. At the end of the day you have a choice, well, you do unless you have this stuck negative core belief: *I am not allowed to choose/decide*... which many people do have.

A life event is likely to have been the reason why you started smoking in the first place: deaths, relationship breakdowns, a controlling grown-up at home. When you get to the root negative core belief linked to that and clear it, you start to feel differently towards smoking. Some people don't want to stop. They have a fear of who they will be without smoking. Well, you'll be the same person, won't you, but without the fags/vaper. If you stop eating crisps, it doesn't change who you are. Smoking somehow feels different, as people smoke to relax, and those same people smoke for many other reasons. They smoke when they are stressed, when they wake up, when they want a breather from the family and just need to go outside and have 5 minutes. People forget that you can go outside and have 5 minutes to yourself with or without smoking. Sometimes it feels like you need to have a reason to have time alone. For those people feeling guilty for taking time out for themselves then smoking is the perfect excuse. Clear that guilt!

Towards the end of this book, there are some negative core beliefs that can be linked to smoking (as well as other issues), but if you do want to stop, start with the common core beliefs first.

> *"The beliefs and decisions you formed pre-six years' old have become the basis of your thoughts today. What appear to be rational thoughts and decisions on the surface may be built on a foundation of misunderstandings and the decisions of a frightened child. If you find that you are not happy with your life situation and with your health, perhaps it is time to dig down to examine the foundations of the structure."*
>
> Sam Thorpe,
> *META Messages from Your Body*, page 173

We criticise ourselves all the time. Everyone has a different experience of the same things: family, culture, school, friends. And from those experiences we engage with and come up with things that we should be, should do, should have. All these things take into account the 'should' from others and not what the actual wants are from our own lives. It is so easy to get lost in other people's 'shoulds', to the point that you can lose sight of yourself amongst what other people expect or think you should be or do. These 'shoulds' can change into negative core beliefs within our systems.

Inherited patterns

Sometimes you can inherit negative core beliefs. Those words spoken at home that are said so many times that they become part of your makeup, part of your brain programming.

Money doesn't grow on trees can lead to a lack mindset.

I will get depression because it runs in the family – this can be a belief that you have taken on with no understanding why other family members had depression, and before you know it, you own it.

I refer to another piece of science by Dr. Bruce Lipton:

> *"We are the drivers of our own biology, just as I am the driver of this word processing program. We have the ability to edit the data we enter into our biocomputers, just as surely as I can choose the words I type. When we understand how IMPs control biology, we become masters of our fate, not victims of our genes."*
>
> Bruce Lipton Ph.D.,
> *The Biology of Belief,* page 94

IMPs are Integral Membrane Proteins, part of the amazing work by cell biologist Dr. Bruce Lipton.

What Dr. Lipton is explaining here, and throughout his book, is that our cells are ours. The cells that make up our bodies are ours uniquely. Yes, we have inherited some of our make-up from our parents, but we can change that. These cells are changed after a 'life experience', be that a trauma or something unpleasant. At that point, our patterns changed, so we can change them again. There is no scientific evidence to show that there is a limit on how many times you can change your mind. When you change your mind, your body changes.

If you have a negative core belief such as *I am stuck with this depression*, then your body changes to suit that belief.

If you have a positive core belief of *This depression is passing through my system*, then the cells in your body adjust to allow for that.

There are so many limiting beliefs that we have, linked to inherited patterns from our family.

1. **Alcoholism runs in my family so that is why I can't control my drinking.**

Surely, if that were the case a better thought pattern would be:

2. I choose to drink, so I can control my drinking.

In which case, you want to investigate your negative core beliefs and make sure that you don't have any that support statement number 1. That way, you can get underneath what you thought was a family pattern. You might never know the reasons why they drank their lives away, but if you could ask them, I am 99.9% sure that it would have made sense to them in their lives and the life that they were living, with the information and knowledge that they had at that time. If you are struggling with alcohol then it is advisable to seek professional support alongside undertaking your own self-help, especially if you are consuming alcohol every day and feel that you cannot miss a day.

The fact that you are reading this means that you are adding to your knowledge bank to make more informed decisions about your mental health and wellbeing.

Dr. Lipton sums it up quite nicely in his Addendum:

> *"The science revealed in this book defines how beliefs control behaviour and gene activity, and consequently the unfolding of our lives. The chapter on Conscious Parenting describes how most of us unavoidably acquired limiting or self-sabotaging beliefs that were downloaded into our subconscious minds when we were children."*
>
> Bruce Lipton Ph.D.,
> *The Biology of Belief*, page 203

So, without having had any 'life experiences', as a child, we all already have limiting or self-sabotaging beliefs just from being around the grown-ups and the families we are born into.

So, the next time you are thinking, **It's all my fault**, consider that it might not be and that just changing that negative core belief can help you to open up to find the real you underneath all the 'stuff' that you have collected over the years.

The Words, later in this book, show you a way to declutter and get rid, release, let go, or whatever you want to call it. You are freeing yourself of 'stuff' that you no longer need and that your brain is still using as fact when you come to make choices or decisions to take action or not.

Reactions to an outside experience

What you witness, what your senses see, hear, taste and touch can lead to negative core beliefs too. For example, the child who tastes a brussels sprout and decides that it tastes horrible (not always the case, I know some people like them!), forms a negative core belief of **I will never eat a green vegetable again**. Parents can be left bewildered why their child loved broccoli last week and they are now refusing to eat anything green.

Another example: the child who has to stand up to a parent at 4 years old and say, "No, stop it", whatever 'it' is. That child can then grow up thinking they must do everything themselves and that no one is looking out for them. They could have accumulated a huge range of negative core beliefs, including:

I am not safe
I don't trust
Nobody is there for me
I must do everything myself
I can't ask for help

These are huge negative core beliefs that a small 4-year-old may take on. As a grown-up, they become so stuck, so ingrained, that the adult can't remember what it was like not to have those negative core beliefs. As a result, they feel that if they change them then their whole identity is going to change and they won't be themselves. When in fact they will be much more 'themselves' without them and have much more energy.

When your brain is constantly battling with negative core beliefs, it is exhausting and it consumes loads of energy, not to mention illness that can occur because of them.

When you react to a situation, those emotions should come and go. If they are staying with you, that's your system's way of saying "deal with me". Strong reactions that stay, invite you to deal with the old stuck emotions that you are carrying around. They are heavy and use up masses of energy. The next time you react with the same emotion, it is much easier for it to come and go. There is nothing for it to stick to.

I will give you a personal example:

Depression

I suffered from depression from being 11- or 12-years old right up to my mid-30s. With my experience of depression, my conscious brain would say, "I want to get up". However, my subconscious brain, running at its superfast speed, would fire all these reasons to my conscious part of the brain why I couldn't, shouldn't, or wasn't good enough, so that by 4pm on the same day I still hadn't moved out of bed or the house. That was some days – for other days I was fully functioning, and could I operate at full pelt for quite a while until I would burn myself out. That cycle played out for years and years.

That is just one simple example of how depression gets hold of you. There are so many negative core beliefs linked to this illness, including:

I will always have this (because someone in authority said so)

I will have to manage life with this (because someone said so)

This is mine (because you decided to take ownership of it)

With these negative core beliefs, or others just as powerful, at the root – let's call them the ringleaders – it is a hard struggle to get anywhere because each time, your brain defaults to *I will always have this, I have to put up with it, I must learn to manage it*, etc.

I then got **post-natal depression** after the birth of my little girl in 2015. Both men and women can be affected by post-natal depression. What was interesting this time (from a practitioner point of view) was that with *the* depression (not mine, the) out of the way and no longer affecting me, I was able to experience post-natal depression in all its glory.

This time my conscious mind was saying *I can't*... change a nappy, look after my baby, do this alone. My partner at that time worked away so I was home alone. My conscious mind was saying *I can't*. This time my subconscious kicked in with, **Yes you can, you can do this**, and it reminded me of all the things I could do. It was my support, not my critic. So, our subconscious holds all the good stuff as well as the bad stuff.

Now, what also struck me, like a bolt of lightning, was that if you are struggling with both depression and post-natal depression then you are stuck, like completely stuck. Your conscious brain is saying *I want to* and *I can't* at the same time as your subconscious brain is saying *I can't* and *I can* simultaneously.

We all have hundreds of negative core beliefs. If you wrote down all of yours, it would be a long list. The good news is that you don't need to tackle each and every one. If you approach them in the right order, you can find that others dissolve away. Deal with the ringleaders and those that have taken up room in your brain by buddying up with the ringleaders. When they go, they have no root in life experience, they are hangers-on.

So, finding a way to identify and manage core beliefs is crucial to our mental health and wellbeing.

> *"Many psychologists have interpreted depression as suppressed anger; Freud, tellingly, described depression as anger redirected against oneself. Now we know something about what this looks like at a cellular level."*
> Candace Pert, Ph.D.,
> *Molecules of Emotion*, page 192

Depression can be the suppression of anger and a whole host of other emotions and stuck negative core beliefs that we decided to keep after experiencing various life events.

From the moment we start life we start collecting core beliefs and emotions. If the grown-ups around you when they were growing up didn't know how to deal with their own emotions, then how can they show you how to deal with yours?

We start to believe what others tell us. As we grow older, we might find out that they lied, or just didn't know, so they fibbed. Either way, you made decisions based on misinformation.

We were born with no limits and then we accumulate life experiences which limit our limitlessness.

We grow, we learn, we experience, and we accumulate more core beliefs.

Our beliefs become outdated, but we hang onto them. The way we think, behave, and feel and react are down to these little sentences. We think we are the way we are and that there is nothing we can do about it.

We can't change our past experiences but we can change what is stuck in our subconscious mind which has our conscious mind believing all sorts of things that are just not right for us in the here and now.

Changing a negative core belief does not change the wise stuff you have learned from your life experiences. If you had a bad relationship breakdown and let go of the negative core beliefs and emotions from that experience, that does not leave you more vulnerable to another bad relationship. You will still be wiser and still see the signs and make better choices for yourself.

However, hanging onto those negative core beliefs becomes limiting so that you don't let anyone get too close for the fear of being hurt. You ensure that you won't get hurt because you don't let anyone near. Just like you won't experience love because you are limiting yourself through your core beliefs.

Triggers

Triggers can cause a reaction. What is a trigger? A trigger is something that consciously or subconsciously reminds you of a trauma or unpleasant life event. Sam Thorpe explains it beautifully here:

> *"Often, we are not aware what our triggers are. We are only aware of how we feel when we have been triggered. This is because at the time of a trauma the subconscious mind will take a snapshot of everything in our surroundings (all sights, smells, sounds and energies) and it will also identify and record everything that is present in our internal system at the time (all foods, chemicals, etc). The subconscious mind now has a record of potential dangers that it wishes to avoid in the future, because they may cause the same reaction as the original trauma. So, when the subconscious encounters a situation that bears similarities to our original traumatic event, it 'triggers' or sets off a warning or protective response in the body. Very often, however, you may not be aware what the connection is between the reaction that you have now and the original traumatic event – it might be any one of the elements captured by the subconscious snapshot. This is also the mechanism through which we develop allergies and intolerances."*
>
> Sam Thorpe,
> *META Messages from Your Body*, page 23

So, here's an example. When I was training in 2009 to be an EFT Practitioner, we were given a demo of how favourites such as chocolate, crisps and cake can hold all sorts of things, including being a trigger. One of the girls said she opens a large bag of crisps and must eat them all. She said it is like a compulsion and that she couldn't stop herself. A short time later, the tutor got to the bottom of it.

When this lady was a child, her father had died. He had passed away around Christmas, so there were lots of goodies around. Because she was a child, no one talked to her about the death of her father and she overheard things like, "She's just a child." This was her father, and no one thought they should be talking to her about what had happened. The crisps were in her 'snapshot'. They were something familiar that reminded her of her father, and all this time, the child, young girl and now the woman had not been able to grieve.

We sat with her whilst the tears came flooding out and it was a privilege to see her transform in front of our eyes. It was a powerful moment for us all and a wonderful realisation for the lady.

Food intolerances and eating habits can be linked to all sorts of life events. Unraveling the issues you find yourself having today can be a great way to start to put past life events in the past, with no emotional attachment or trigger in the present day.

Triggers are not only linked to food. As the brain takes a snapshot of your environment during a traumatic event or time, then seemingly unconnected things such as fears of fish, buttons, zips, pictures, lights, and also textures and smells can be triggers. Many fears can be triggers linked to past 'stuff'.

I worked with a lady some time ago who came to me with a fear of flying. We had just two sessions and it was surprising to the client what happened. We talked about her fear of flying. We talked about the whole process and where the panic started to rise. We talked the whole experience through, from booking the holiday to parking at the airport, checking in, walking to the security, passport control, boarding, and walking to the plane.

As we talked about it, we got through handing in the boarding passes and then the panic started to rise. The client said that, after handing in the boarding pass, as she walked down the tube towards the plane she started to panic. This was vivid in her recall of the thought. She also said it reminded her of being in a lift. As soon as I heard that I said, "OK, let's forget about the plane for now and tell me about your fear of lifts".

What the client in fact had was a fear of lifts. When we cleared that fear, she was geared up and ready and wanted to get in a lift there and then. I went back to talk about the plane and the fear of flying, and she just laughed and said, "That's ridiculous, I don't have a fear of flying, how daft is that!" Just to be certain, I then got the client to visualise the whole process of getting to the airport and getting onto the plane. This time we imagined it all the way to her seat and take off as well as landing. So, the fear of lifts was the issue, but the 'snapshot' that was taken around the fear of lifts raised its head when the environment was similar to that of a lift.

Our brains are so clever, aren't they? Sometimes we do need to give them a good mucking out to clear out the outdated stuff. If you don't let go of past issues, your brain will replay them over and over, so just ignoring them or saying you are blocking them just makes them more stuck. Dealing with emotions and negative core beliefs prevents them from developing and steering your behaviour. Even when you ignore emotions and negative core beliefs or consciously push them away, your subconscious doesn't.

Oh, just think positive?? No, that's not going to do it either, as these little nuggets, monkeys, limiters, whatever you call your negative core beliefs, are there to stay unless you ask them to leave.

In 1997, the research that Candace Pert was doing was bang on. 23 years later, today in 2020 (at the time of writing this book), it is still bang on. We need to initiate some radical change to help people, and that can start with every individual doing their own bit of self-care each week or month. It doesn't need to take long: 20- to 30-minutes a week, and the more you start to feel better, the more you want to clear out. The biggest hurdles are discovering how to do it, making a commitment and taking those first steps. If we all take responsibility for ourselves, we can grow into a happier and healthier society.

> *"If everyone's so happy, why is depression at near-epidemic proportions in our society? Are we all in denial, clinging to what we believe is the cultural norm, what is socially expected of us? Are we ashamed to admit we might be sad, unhappy, disappointed, and not altogether satisfied with life?"*
> Candace Pert, Ph.D.,
> *Molecules of Emotion*, page 264, 265

I have worked with clients who tell me that they can't admit how they feel because if they do so, they feel that their whole world is going to crumble, and that they themselves are the only glue holding everything together. In fact, if they took the time to deal with their stuff, the world would not stop. The world would carry on, and other people, once aware of their situation, would begin to help. That first step around asking for help is so difficult because it is probably the first time you have said out loud how you feel.

When you ask for help out loud it feels different in your mind and body. So, before you ask for help, practise what you will say to yourself. Be with yourself and say those words out loud. When you come to say it to your friends or family it is already familiar, and you will know how it feels. Saying things out loud makes a big difference.

People can often feel like they are out of control. Control of a situation is a big issue, especially for those people who felt controlled as a child. They feel if they let go then they will lose control.

Other people I have helped have a belief that you need to have some of each negative emotion in your system to function correctly. This is codswallop; I'm not actually sure what codswallop is but now I've checked, I can say that it is... nonsense. Emotions are signals that tell you how you are feeling. Emotions are your reactions to a situation. We don't need to hoard or keep any emotions to know how they feel. If you release all the anger out of your body and mind from past events, it doesn't stop you from feeling anger in the future, nor do you forget how to feel anger.

Holding any negative emotion in your mind and body is only harmful. It sits and it festers and then it buddies up with other emotions and starts to make you think that things are always bad. Moment to moment, going forward with these negative emotions still lingering, they will be forced forward so that when you *do* feel angry that anger is intensified. So, if you are feeling anger in the moment, the here and now, you'll have the addition of past anger linked back to memories.

We don't need to carry old stuff around – it's like wearing new clothes and wearing old clothes at the same time. Would you wear the clothes you wore when you were 6 years old in your 20s or 30s? No, I wouldn't either, so why do we all feel that we need to carry all these old emotions around with us?

> *"My research has shown me that when emotions are expressed – which is to say that the biochemicals that are the substrate of emotion are flowing freely – all systems are united and made whole. When emotions are repressed, denied, not allowed to be whatever they may be, our network pathways get blocked, stopping the flow of the vital feel-good, unifying chemicals that run both our biology and our behaviour."*
>
> Candace Pert, Ph.D.,
> *Molecules of Emotion*, page 273

So, there we go. Our bodies don't work properly if we hold emotions in and in turn, this affects our behaviour. To follow this up, Candace Pert goes on to say:

> *"However, if our emotions are blocked due to denial, repression, or trauma, then blood flow can become chronically constricted, depriving the frontal cortex, as well as other organs, of vital nourishment. This can leave you foggy and less alert... As a result, you may become stuck – unable to respond freshly to the world around you, repeating old patterns of behaviour and feelings that are responses to an outdated knowledge base."*
>
> Candace Pert, Ph.D.,
> *Molecules of Emotion*, page 289

Feeling safe

When you start to go through the lists in this book, you need to say the core beliefs out loud. As you start to use **The Words** you will start to release old stuff you no longer need. Mostly you will be happy for it to go. It feels safe. If you don't feel safe there will be a reason for this – this is where you need to turn Miss Marple or Poirot and undertake some detective work.

There are some emotions and negative core beliefs where you might not feel safe in letting them go, and this can happen for all sorts of reasons.

There might be an underlying reason why it doesn't feel safe. This can sometimes be when a negative core belief has been with you for so long it begins to feel like it is you, and to let it go feels like you are getting rid of part of yourself.

Sometimes, people feel like they will change or be different and not themselves when, in fact, the opposite is true. By releasing stuck emotions, you get back to being the real true you.

If you don't feel safe doing this for yourself then it is advisable to see a practitioner – there is a practitioner list on my website.

When they have helped you with the safety side, you can then do most, if not all, of the releasing of emotions and negative core beliefs for yourself, just by using this book.

You might also want to try clearing the negative core belief of *I am not safe*... as well as the emotions that come up around that.

Buddying up

Emotions and negative core beliefs buddy up and support each other. Many times, there are emotions attached to a negative core belief. Here is an example:

If you have a fear, that fear can be linked to all sorts of things:

- of failure
- of death
- of life
- of success

The negative core beliefs within that fear include:

I always fail
I will always fail
I am a failure
I can't get it right
I am useless

Another example could be that while dealing with the negative core belief, *I am not safe*, the following emotions may be supporting that negative core belief:

Trust
Sadness
Blame

Despair
Humiliation

The list goes on...

A pair of core beliefs shows a positive and a negative statement, such as: *I can* and *I can't*. Pairs of core beliefs can be around all sorts of subjects, for example, money:

I love money
I don't love money

If you believed both of these statements, you would be stuck in a loop and probably skint too, or find that you get money only for it to be in one hand and out of the other. There are many negative core beliefs to explore around money, although by clearing the above it won't on its own make you rich. It is just a start to working out where your blocks and limiting beliefs are. However, it might be that your new empowered and more positive actions make you rich as a result of clearing the limits of negative core beliefs that were holding you back from taking action.

Ownership

Many people, unbeknown to themselves, have taken ownership of their emotions, negative core beliefs, and illnesses. Taking ownership means that somewhere in your subconscious you are comfortable and have taken on board that you will always have the emotions, or that trauma will always raise its head, or that you will always have to deal with that illness.

With illness, emotions and negative core beliefs can get stuck. You might be struggling to deal with those emotions and negative core beliefs, or maybe they are buried and packed away so much that you have forgotten they are there or didn't even realise that they were there. These stuck emotions and negative core beliefs can present themselves in the body as illness or pain. Some emotions find their comfy places and their regular spots to hide in. When my shoulders start to feel stiff, I know something is lurking. I get my list out and get rid of whatever is in there squatting!!

Sam Thorpe's research says it beautifully:

> *"If emotions are not processed or released, they will be embodied in illness. Then you have the emotions as well as the physical or mental illness. Perhaps if you could understand your emotions, you could use them as your internal guidance system, rather than be fearful and suppress them with all the consequences that entails."*
>
> Sam Thorpe,
> *META Messages from Your Body*, page 23

By releasing stuck emotions and negative core beliefs you can begin to feel and understand your emotions in a different way. So, as Sam says, start to use them as your internal guidance system.

Vows

Vows can be similar to negative core beliefs, but vows are usually statements which start *I will never... I do...* Generally, these are spoken out loud either on your own or in front of family or friends. Vows you will be familiar with are marriage vows, but what about divorce vows? How many of us say separation vows so that we are not energetically connected to another person? Not many, and so we still feel a certain amount of control and connection to them.

For example, let's look at the vow you take during a marriage ceremony: *I do*. What about when a marriage ceases to be a marriage? You have, at some point, made a vow about that too and it is important to undo that vow. You can do this using the power of words. Following the breakdown of a relationship, you might say something like:

I will never trust anyone

You might say that when a relationship has broken down, but that isn't dealing with the situation. That is just adding more limiting beliefs to your hard drive. Not trusting anyone is a reaction to the life event.

We can make vows about other things too. What about a girl at 20 years old, who stands in her bedroom announcing to herself, the world, and no one in particular: "I will never love anyone."

Why, you might ask? Here is what was going on in her life at that time:

- She was struggling with depression
- She had final exams at University looming in only a few weeks
- Her dad had walked out
- Her grandmother died a few weeks after that
- She had a 21st birthday party to look forward to

The hurt she was feeling from the deaths and departure of her family made her feel like it wasn't worth it. It wasn't worth loving anyone because they will just leave you anyway.

She was struggling, really struggling, and so in order to make some sense of her grandmother's death and her dad walking out, she decided it was going to be much easier if she didn't love anyone, EVER. That way she couldn't get hurt.

She lived out that vow too well, so that by the time she had cleared and released that vow, she already had two failed marriages, a fiancée plus a string of non-relationships behind her. She was so ready for that vow to go, and what a relief it was for her.

Now she loves everyone and is in a much better situation. I am talking about love as in 'love', not as in I am 'in love'/relationship with everyone. That would be exhausting in a different way!!

After uncovering that vow, we also uncovered this belief:

I can't have friends who are boys

Before her dad left she had friends who were boys. One of her best friends was a boy. She went to university with him. However, after her dad left with one of her mum's friends, she didn't see much of her friend who is a boy. She put it down to things changing and university ending. They didn't see each other, although they still lived close to one another. That negative core belief, mixed with that vow, meant that every time she got friendly with a boy, she thought she had to have a relationship with them. It made her awkward around her friends' boyfriends. She felt like it was wrong to talk to them as friends. Whether they knew it or not, it was such a strong negative core belief and interlinked so much with relationships. Now, she has healthy positive core beliefs linked to healthy relationships and is doing great. She is single and has friends who are boys... result!!

Do you see how powerful, 3, 4, 5, 6 or 7 little words can be? There is so much that can be beneath their meaning, and, in turn, they affect so much about how we behave in life.

PART TWO

Chapter 4
The Power of Words

In this chapter, I am going to introduce you to lists. I am going to show you the words you can use to release and let go of stuck emotions and negative core beliefs. Further on in the chapter you will find out the how.

A note on responsibility: Please take responsibility for your own wellbeing should you choose to use *The Words*.

IMPORTANT

As you go through your emotions and negative core beliefs and start to clear them away, you will start to feel better in yourself, pretty much straightaway. The following are **important** things to remember:

- If you are on any medication, **do not just stop taking your medication.** Work with your doctor and explain what you have been doing and ask them to help you safely withdraw from your medication.

- **Allow yourself some time,** what I like to call 'Quality Blankie Time' (QBT), after you have cleared some negative core beliefs. This is time to lie on the sofa or in bed, set your alarm for an hour and allow yourself to get comfy. Watch some TV, eat something you like, get your duvet or a blanket and keep yourself warm and then snooze or just be there. If you feel guilty for doing this, clear that guilt away. You are worth it, and **you don't have to be ill to have a duvet day or duvet hour.** If there is someone at home who will react to you doing this, then take yourself off for a walk or find a safe and quiet place to sit. If you have a friend you can ask, go and sit at their house, relax and **be kind to yourself.**

- To start with, **try clearing three or four emotions/negative core beliefs** and then give yourself a breather before trying to do more. They may be only small sentences, but they are powerful. These short sentences have been running the show for a long time, so give yourself a bit of time to process.

- **Say *The Words* out loud.** Saying the emotion and the negative core belief out loud helps you to identify with it. Have you ever prepared something in your head and then when you started saying it out loud it sounds like a load of rubbish and not at all as you prepared it? Saying things out loud allows you to notice how that feels in your mind and body. It is also important to say *The Words* out loud so that you can hear yourself saying them. When you say things in your head, it is easy to con yourself that it isn't one of your emotions or negative core beliefs. **It is important we hear ourselves out loud.**

- When you **say *The Words* out loud, notice how it feels.** Do they feel true, false or somewhere in-between? You might notice that feeling somewhere in your body too. Just be aware of it, be aware of your mind and body working together.

- If you have strong emotions or strong reactions, you might like to **work with a friend, a support or with a professional practitioner** to help you.

- If you and a friend are reading this book, **buddying up together to clear things out can be a great support.** This can be done via video call or face-to-face, so it doesn't matter where your book buddy lives.

- **Be kind to yourself!**

Memories, flashbacks & other emotions

Sometimes, as you are clearing one thing away, you might get a random memory that you haven't thought about for a long time. You might think it isn't relevant, but if it comes to mind, it is highly likely to be linked to the negative core belief or emotion that you are clearing.

If you can or cannot associate it with anything, it really doesn't matter.

If the memory or flashback raises a negative emotion, then write that emotion down and clear that negative emotion away. This is normal – your brain will be giving you memories that still contain an intensity of emotion so you can clear the emotion.

Pairs of core beliefs

Creating pairs of statements for balancing up a core belief helps when pairs of core beliefs are out of sync. The process is the same: say each core belief, the positive statement and the negative statement out loud and see how it feels: true, false or somewhere in-between. Here is an example:

I don't trust – feels true or in-between when you say it out loud

I do trust – feels false or in-between when you say it out loud

What you are aiming for is:

I don't trust = feels false when you say it out loud

I do trust = feels true when you say it out loud

By balancing and changing your core belief to that of trusting people does not mean that others can then walk all over you. You still have the memory, but without the emotions or negative core belief. Learning to trust again doesn't need to be a long and painful experience. You will however make much wiser choices going forward, based on your experience.

Your lists

As you start to look through your lists, you might at a glance think, "Oh my god, I have all of these", and that might be the case, but you don't have to go through them all. As I have mentioned before, as soon as you find one belief, deal with that one. If it is a ringleader, you will find that other negative core beliefs dissolve away just from doing this one.

So, there is no need to feel overwhelmed. Just doing a few of them a week, which is what, around 20 or 30 minutes of your time, you can start to feel so much better in mind and body. You will also find that the words that were stuck have been so powerful in how you react to situations that you find yourself reacting in a much better way for you. There are just so many benefits to sorting out those words.

The following pages show you the key words that we can say out loud to release the emotions and to change the negative core beliefs we are hanging onto.

How to use *The Words*

The Words are in the next section and are repeated on the last page of the book for easy reference. Here is how to use them:

1. Look at the list of emotions/negative core beliefs.

2. Either start at the top of the list or see which ones jump out at you from the page.

3. Say that emotion/negative core belief out loud.

4. Don't race ahead, deal with one at a time.

5. Feel how that emotion/negative core belief feels when you say "My system is holding onto… [state emotion/negative core belief]" Does that feel true, false, or somewhere in-between for you?

6. If true or somewhere in-between, go to step 7. If false, then go to Step 1 to find the next emotion or negative core belief and repeat the process.

7. Say *The Words* out loud to help you to release emotions/negative core beliefs.

8. Take a deep breath.

9. If any other emotions came to mind while you were saying *The Words*, write them down and use *The Words* for each of those too.

10. Go back to your original emotion/negative core belief and say, "My system is holding onto... *[state emotion/negative core belief]*" See how that feels: true, false, or somewhere in-between.

11. If true or somewhere in-between, go to step 7. If false, then go to Step 1 to find the next emotion or negative core belief and repeat the process.

At this point, if you have cleared a few emotions/negative core beliefs, you might need a bit of Quality Blankie Time.

It is important not to take on too much in one go. Allow yourself time to process things and don't underestimate how much energy it takes to release something that has been stuck for many years. Once processed, you may find that you have more energy, because your system (mind and body), which has been fighting with those emotions, using up precious energy, now has a bit more free time.

Other side effects, as well as feeling tired, may be feeling hungry, yawning a lot and going to the loo a little more than normal.

It is important to keep hydrated and warm.

The following pages give you a series of lists. These are lists of common emotions that we all feel, experience, keep, and sometimes need to let go of.

There are lists of common negative core beliefs, followed by more negative core beliefs that can be linked to things such as weight management or stopping smoking. It is important to understand that these negative core beliefs, although under the heading of Weight Management or Stop Smoking, can be linked to many other things as well. So even if you don't want to stop smoking or manage your weight, have a look through those lists too. They can be linked to anyone for anything. I have put them under those headings just to show you how many things can be linked to our behaviours and actions.

PLEASE NOTE: There are zillions of core beliefs. The lists here are not all the core beliefs in the world. So, if you think of one that isn't listed, write it in the book, add it to the list (unless this is a library book of course!!). I have left some extra lines at the end of the lists for you to add your own.

Chapter 5

The Words

OK, here are **The Words.** Refer to Steps 1-11 on page 75. The steps are repeated on the last page of this book for ease of reference.

What we are going to do is say a word or a small sentence (a negative core belief) out loud. This is our conscious mind asking our subconscious mind: **What do you think?**

As you say the word or small sentence out loud you will get a feeling as to whether the word or words are true, false, or somewhere in-between. This is your subconscious mind and body telling your conscious mind the truth of what is stored.

Then, our conscious mind is going to read some words in which we ask the subconscious to make some changes. As I mentioned earlier, our subconscious waits to be asked. It is a hoarder of emotions and comments that it has heard and observed. So, we ask it.

- We say the words,
- wait a minute or so,
- take a few deep breaths
- and see how we are doing.

We are taking control; we are minding our mind. It is your brain and even though you don't think you are thinking with your subconscious, you are, all the time. So, I think it's nice to get it involved, don't you?

There are a few different ways that you can do this. Personally, when I find a negative core belief, I just get rid of the negative. Some people like to balance up the negative statement with a positive statement. So, my lovelies, you have a choice, or you can mix it up and use a combination.

A few pointers

To start with, you might be tempted to crack on and take on loads of negative core beliefs and have a good old clear out. As tempting as that is, it is good to start with three or four, maybe five per week or every three or four days. Some of these negative core beliefs are linked to so much stuff that has gone on in our lives that when they untangle, it can be tiring. We all need to function day-to-day, so be kind to yourself and don't overdo it or you might find you are wiped out.

If you have drunk alcohol the words won't work in the same way! Then it's too easy to tell yourself things that aren't true and not connect properly with yourself.

It can be tiring or exhilarating. Either way, after you have cleared a few negative core beliefs, give yourself a bit of Quality Blankie Time (QBT) to help you to process it all and take stock. You have been carrying some of this 'stuff' around with you for a long time. It gets heavy, so don't be surprised if your eyes close and you find yourself succumbing to nice little nap. QBT may also mean for you; taking a little walk, sitting under a tree, lying in the garden, if you are lucky enough to have one. If you haven't, why not just find a green space in which to sit and just be. I do this, sometimes with a hot chocolate.

EMOTIONS – THE WORDS

Say these words out loud:

> **Even though I feel...** *[state the emotion]*
>
> I am asking my subconscious to release this now.
>
> I am asking my subconscious to release what needs to be released, and change what needs to change, so my conscious mind doesn't have to.
>
> That was then, this is now.
>
> That emotion of... *[state emotion]* is no longer working for me.
>
> Releasing... *[state emotion]* safely and completely, through all space and time and throughout my whole system.

Now you have completed that section, take a deep breath, give yourself a few minutes before checking back with yourself, or moving onto the next one.

Say the emotion out loud again and feel its intensity. If you can still feel it, say the words again or have a look at the list. There might be something else linked to it.

Always good to drink water whilst doing this.

CORE BELIEFS – THE WORDS

Say these words out loud:

Even though I have this core belief... *[state core belief]*

I am now choosing to release this.

I am asking my subconscious to release this now.

I am asking my subconscious to release what needs to release, and change what needs to change, so my conscious mind doesn't have to.

That was then, this is now.

That core belief of... *[state core belief]* is no longer working for me.

Releasing... *[state core belief]* safely and completely, through all space and time and throughout my whole system.

Now you have completed that section, take a deep breath, give yourself a few minutes before checking back with yourself, and if any memories or flashbacks came up, write down what they are and then tackle them one at a time.

If you don't recall any emotions, memories or flashbacks, then that's fine. I very rarely get flashbacks; I trust that my superfast subconscious is dealing with it.

Say the negative core belief out loud again and feel if it is true, false, or somewhere in-between. It is normal for some people to not know what they think about that statement. If that is the case, sleep on it and say it again out loud the following day after you have woken up. How does it feel then?

Always good to drink water whilst doing this.

CORE BELIEF BALANCE
– THE WORDS

Say these words out loud:

Even though I have these core beliefs... *[state the pair of core beliefs, e.g. I can, I can't]*

I am now choosing to release these.

I am asking my subconscious to unravel this now.

I am asking my subconscious to release what needs to release, and change what needs to change, so my conscious mind doesn't have to.

That was then, this is now.

I am asking for those core beliefs of... *[state the pair of core beliefs]* to be brought back into a healthy balance.

Releasing what is not working for me safely and completely, through all space and time, and throughout my whole system.

Now you have completed that section, take a deep breath, give yourself a few minutes before checking back with yourself, and if any memories or flashbacks came up, write down what they are and then tackle them one at a time.

Again, if you don't recall any emotions, memories or flashbacks then that's fine. I very rarely get flashbacks, as I trust that my superfast subconscious is dealing with it.

State the pair of core beliefs out loud again and feel each one in turn, to see if it is true, false, or somewhere in-between. It is normal for some people to not know what they think about that statement, so, in that case, sleep on it and say it again out loud the following day after you have woken up. How does it feel then?

Always good to drink water whilst doing **The Words**.

The following pages show the lists of emotions and core beliefs that you can read through (out loud) and which you can come back to time and time again, to see which ones feel strong to you.

When we are on the receiving end of others' actions, this makes us feel a certain way. Our brains take in a snapshot of all the information that we can see and experience at that time when people said or did mean things to us. People intentionally say mean things to us, and we take those words on board. People say words to us that they intend to be kind, but we receive them differently and interpret them in accordance with the life events that we have experienced. When we say words out loud, we hear them ourselves and it is in this time and space that we need to hear ourselves and feel how these words are in our systems. If you have out-of-date food in your cupboard, you chuck it out. Same thing here: outdated emotions and negative core beliefs need to go, because if you keep experiencing them over and over they are going to make you ill and behave in a way that limits your enjoyment of life.

Our brains are our body's computer.

You may feel great benefits in your body as you unravel the limiting beliefs holding you back.

If you start to 'Mind Your Mind' regularly, it is normal for the same emotion to crop up a few times. This is normal. Persevere and if you find it frustrating, clear the frustration. It could be that a core belief is hanging onto or underpinning the emotion that keeps raising its head, so a good idea is to check out your core beliefs too.

This is an exciting time.

Enjoy the process and feeling the joy that emerges as you get back to the real you, the best version of you without all the 'stuff' that you have taken on board, and that other people have put there.

Happy days xx

Chapter 6

EMOTIONS: Your List

A list of emotions:

Abandonment	Disgusted	Impatient
Afraid	Dread	Indecisiveness
Aggression		Insecurity
Anger	Effort unreceived	Irritated
Annoyed	Embarrassment	Isolated
Anxiety		
Ashamed	Failure	Jealousy
	Fear	
Betrayal	Forlorn	Lack of control
Bitterness	Forgiveness	Lonely
Blame	Frustration	Longing
		Lost
Conflict	Grief	Love unreceived
Confusion	Grumpy	Low self-esteem
Creative insecurity	Guilt	Lust
Crying		
	Hatred	Miserable
Deceitful	Heartache	Mournful
Defensive	Helplessness	
Depressed	Hopelessness	Nervous
Despair	Horror	
Disappointment	Humiliation	Offended
Discouragement	Hurt	Overjoy

Overwhelm	Self-abuse	Unhappy
	Selfishness	Unsupported
Panic	Shame	Unworthy
Peeved	Shock	
Pity	Sorrow	Vulnerable
Pride	Spiteful	
	Stressful	Wishy-washy
Regret	Stubbornness	Worthless
Rejection		Worry
Resentment	Taken for granted	
	Terror	
Sadness	Truth	

List additional emotions that come up for you here:

_____

_____

_____

_____

_____

_____

_____

_____

_____

_____

_____

_____

_____

_____

_____

_____

_____

_____

_____

_____

_____

Chapter 7
CORE BELIEFS: Common

Here is a comprehensive list of common positive core beliefs with their opposite, the equivalent negative core belief. Other words can be used as opposites/positives but for the purposes of this, it is important to use words as close to the original negative core belief as possible.

The simpler you can make the words, the better the changes to the subconscious. If you try to make it too complicated by choosing exact opposites, it doesn't send the clear message to your subconscious and can create a watered-down version of what you are trying to fix in the first place. Be clear. If you feel you can't be clear, you might like to try clearing the following pair before continuing:

I always complicate things – I do not always complicate things.

People have different ways of saying things and give a slightly different interpretation to what some words mean. So, if you are reading through them and are not sure about a specific word but have a different word that you use, then change it. Use your words and use what you understand and are comfortable with. For example, some people don't like to say 'heal', so you might choose to say 'mend' instead, or an equivalent word which you prefer.

If you say to yourself, *I am p*ssed off* then that's a negative core belief, so you can say, **I am p*ssed off – I am not p*ssed off.** Just because it contains a swear word doesn't mean you can't use it. We all use swear words for different reasons. They are words, so if they are included in your self-talk, then go for it. Use it with **The Words,** so you don't feel p*ssed off!

I just deal with the negative core belief which is what you may prefer to do. If you want to deal with both the positive and the negative then you will need **The Words** for the 'Core Belief Balance'. Find what works for you.

If you do have any of your own, you can add them in the blank boxes towards the end of this section.

Enjoy the process!

Negative core belief	Opposite/positive core belief
I am of no value	I am of value
I don't care for myself	I care for myself
I am useless	I am not useless
I don't like me	I like me / I love me
I don't deserve	I do deserve
It's always my fault	It's not all my fault
I am always unhappy	I can be happy
I can never be happy	I can be happy
I always worry	I never worry
I always feel guilty	I never feel guilty
I want to die	I want to live
I am not good enough	I am good enough
It is always my fault	It is not always my fault
I am worthless	I am not worthless
I am rubbish	I am not rubbish
I am not worthy	I am worthy
I am not worth anything to anyone	I am worth something to myself and to others

Negative core belief	Opposite/positive core belief
I am no good	I am good
I can't ever put myself first	I can put myself first
I am not important	I am important
I am nothing	I am not nothing
I have nothing to offer	I have lots to offer
Nobody values me	I value me
Nobody cares about me	I care about me
People who say nice things to me don't mean them	I can believe nice things about myself
I am stupid	I am not stupid
I always get it wrong	I don't always get it wrong
I am flawed	I am not flawed
I will fail	I will not fail
I am powerless	I am powerful
I am incompetent	I am not incompetent
I can't do anything right	I can do things right
I can't get it right	I can get it right
I am not any good	I am good
I am unsuccessful	I am successful
I am inferior	I am not inferior
I am a failure	I am not a failure
I am a loser	I am not a loser
I always lose	I don't always lose
I don't deserve to be loved	I deserve to be loved
I don't deserve to be cared for	I deserve to be cared for
I don't deserve anything	I do deserve
I don't exist	I do exist
I am invisible	I am not invisible
I am insignificant	I am not insignificant
I am not enough	I am enough
I am not recognised	I am recognised
I am unlovable	I am lovable
I am unacceptable	I am acceptable
I am always left out	I am not always left out

Negative core belief	Opposite/positive core belief
I don't matter	I do matter
I am not special	I am special
I am not wanted	I am wanted
I am alone	I am not alone
I am unwelcome	I am welcome
I can never be loved	I can be loved
I am defective	I am not defective
I am bad	I am not bad
I am broken	I am not broken
I am unfixable	I can be repaired
I am unrepairable	I can be repaired
I cannot be healed	I can be healed
I am doomed	I am not doomed
I am going to die early in life	I am not going to die early
I am damaged	I am not damaged
I am mentally defective	I am not mentally defective
I am emotionally crippled	I am not emotionally crippled
I am emotionally defective	I am not emotionally defective
I will always have mental problems	I will not always have mental problems
I always hurt	I don't always hurt
I am always in pain	I am not always in pain
Nobody can heal my pain	I can heal
I am not whole	I am whole
I have no integrity	I have integrity
I have no hope	I have hope
I feel hopeless	I do not feel hopeless
I have lost my spirit	I have not lost my spirit
Nothing good ever happens to me	Good things can happen to me
I can't ever believe in myself	I believe in myself
I am not safe	I am safe
I never feel safe	I can feel safe
Everything is a struggle	Everything is not a struggle

Negative core belief	Opposite/positive core belief
I don't fit in	I do fit in
I always feel lost	I do not always feel lost
I am always alone	I am not always alone
I have never been wanted	I am wanted
I should never have been born	I was born for a reason
I was always a mistake	I am not a mistake
I am a mistake	I am not a mistake
I am not welcome	I am welcome
I have never felt safe	I can feel safe
I am not protected	I am protected
I am always afraid	I am not always afraid
I can't do anything myself	I can do things myself
I always feel vulnerable	I don't always feel vulnerable
I always feel helpless	I don't always feel helpless
I can never help myself	I can help myself
Nobody can help me	I can be helped
I will never be able to fix it	I can fix it
I can't fix it	I can fix it
I can't trust	I can trust
I always feel judged	I don't always feel judged
I can't forgive myself	I can forgive myself
I will never forgive them	I can forgive them
I am always manipulated by others	I am not always manipulated by others
It's all their fault	It's not all their fault
I always feel controlled by others	I am not controlled by others
I feel trapped	I am not trapped
I do not trust myself	I trust myself
Nobody trusts me	I am trusted
Nobody trusts me to do anything right	I am trusted
I can't control anything	I can control things
I can't achieve	I can achieve

Negative core belief	Opposite/positive core belief
I can't change	I can change
I have no options	I have options
I always fail	I don't always fail
I always get it wrong	I don't always get it wrong
I am always wrong	I am not always wrong
I always feel confused	I am not always confused
I am not trustworthy	I am trustworthy
I can't trust people	I can trust people
I never trust others	I can trust others
I have no control	I have control
I am out of control	I am not out of control
I can't make it work	I can make it work
I can't	I can
I am not allowed to be me	I am allowed to be me
I am never seen or heard	I am seen and heard
I always think the worst	I don't always think the worst
Nobody likes me	I am liked
I don't like me	I like me
I can't cope	I can cope
My life is a struggle	My life is not a struggle
My body is not my friend	My body is my friend
I can't ever get it right	I can get it right
I am awkward	I am not awkward
I don't fit in anywhere	I can fit in
I am never heard	I can be heard
I am unattractive	I am attractive
Everything I do goes wrong	Not everything goes wrong
I always attract bad things	I don't always attract bad things
Nothing ever goes right for me	Things can go right for me
I have ruined my whole life	I have not ruined my whole life
I am always too slow	I am not always too slow
I am in the wrong place	I am not in the wrong place

Negative core belief	Opposite/positive core belief
Wherever I am, I don't like it	Wherever I am, I like it
I am guilty	I am not guilty
It is not safe to be me	It is safe to be me
I am bad	I am not bad
I am a bad person	I am not a bad person
I am not whole	I am whole
I am imperfect	I am perfect
I can't be me	I can be me
I am hopeless	I am not hopeless
I'm dirty	I am not dirty
I am ugly	I am not ugly
I am fat	I am not fat
I am shameful	I am not shameful
I am unclean	I am clean
I am useless	I am not useless
I am a reject	I am not a reject
I am crazy	I am not crazy
I am unbalanced	I am balanced
There's something wrong with me	There is nothing wrong with me
I am not good enough	I am good enough
I'm not right in the head	I am right in the head
I am a fake	I am not a fake
I don't know what is real	I do know what is real
I am unsuitable	I am suitable
I am not true	I am true
I don't know who I really am	I do know who I really am
I am sinful	I am not sinful
I am evil	I am not evil
I can't grow	I can grow
I must not get my hopes up	I can get my hopes up
I can't fix anything	I can fix things
I need someone else to mend me	I can mend me

Negative core belief	Opposite/positive core belief
I need someone else to heal me	I can heal me
I can't get anything right	I can get things right
Everything I try to do goes wrong	Everything I try to do does not go wrong
I am not happy in my own skin	I am happy in my own skin

Chapter 8
CORE BELIEFS:
Weight Acceptance & Management

Here is a list of the negative core beliefs that can be linked to many life events as well as weight management and body acceptance.

The first section deals with core beliefs that can be balanced. The list below shows negative core beliefs directly linked to weight, because we don't always know what weight issues can be linked to. If you feel that, as you are saying these, you need some professional help, please do seek it. There is a list on my website of practitioners who specialise in core belief and emotional work.

Weight can be dictated by stuck emotions, and as soon as you start clearing this stuff, the weight starts to move.

Someone who has experienced a traumatic life event can end up feeling like they don't want to be attractive, so that the same things do not happen to them again. So, in those cases, the weight stays on to keep them safe.

Weight can also be linked to not wanting to be attractive to a possible partner or current partner. Some people who have experienced sexual abuse or mental abuse have been shown or told over and over how worthless they are by the actions and words of other people. If any of that rings true for you, seek professional support before trying to deal with these things, for the first time, alone.

Here's a negative core belief:

There is never enough food

If you have this negative core belief, it can come from a lack of food at home when you were younger. How about those babies that were hungry and never got enough milk? It is not that they were greedy; they were hungry. New mums were frightened of overfeeding, of doing things wrong. This all transfers into **there is never enough food** or **there is never enough.** It may be that there has been a lack of food at home or a lack of something, it doesn't have to be food; it could be clothes, care, money, love… the list is endless. This negative core belief can lead your body and mind to eat and drink more than it needs, as there is then an inbuilt fear that there won't be enough. Naturally, our bodies stock up if they fear a lack. If you miss meals, your body stores up fat because it isn't sure when the next meal might be.

Weight management is not always about losing weight. Sometimes people are struggling to put weight on, so there are core beliefs in there to help with that too.

Some core beliefs relating to weight management:

Negative core belief	Opposite/positive core belief
I can't lose weight	I can lose weight
I don't like my body	I like my body
I don't like me	I like me
I don't accept my weight as it is now	I accept my weight as it is now
I don't want to lose weight	I want to lose weight
I don't believe I can do this	I do believe I can do this
I can't talk about my weight	I can talk about my weight
My weight is stuck	My weight is not stuck
I will always be fat	I won't always be fat
I am giving up	I am not giving up
I will never lose weight	I will lose weight
I can't gain weight	I can gain weight

You may find that these beliefs can bring up all sorts of memories, emotions, and flashbacks. If you feel that you need help, it is advisable to have a session with a professional to help you, and then you can continue to Mind Your Mind. However, you may feel that you can do this yourself. Always remember to give yourself a bit of Quality Blankie Time after you have been clearing core beliefs and emotions, as you need to adjust and process. Doing too much can wipe you out and we all need to be able to function day-to-day.

Here are some common negative core beliefs linked to weight. As you will see, they are just in the negative with no opposite. For these, we just want to be free from them and reap the benefits of being without negative core beliefs limiting our actions and decisions.

Food controls me   I always gain weight

I always lose weight

I always put on weight

I always think about food

I always need to be on a diet

I always put it back on

I always struggle with my weight

I always worry about my weight

I am alone

I am always frustrated about my weight

I am always judged

I am always judged because of how I look

I am always judged because of my weight

I am always left out

I am always rejected

I am always rejected by me

I am always rejected by others

I am always thinking about my weight

I am always worried about what other people do think of me

I can't

I can't be trusted with food

I can't be fat and happy

I can't be thin

I can't be thin and happy

I can't buy clothes that I like

I can't count calories

I can't diet

I can't do anything

I can't do this

I can't eat healthily

I can't ever sort this out

I can't fix anything

I can't forgive myself

I can't have a relationship

I can't have fun

I can't talk about my weight

I don't accept me

I don't care about my appearance

I don't deserve

I don't feel attractive

I don't feel sexy

I feel guilty

I find it hard to lose weight

I find it hard to stay slim

I give up

I hate diets

I hate how I feel

I hate how I look

I hate how my body feels

I hate the extra weight

I hate trying

I have abused my body

I have abused my body with food

I have always struggled with my weight

I have a slow metabolism

I have failed my body

I have given up

I have lost all my confidence

I hide

I let myself down

I loathe my body

I look hideous

I look horrendous

I make myself angry

It's because I have had kids

It's because I have had an operation

It's hard to lose weight

It's in my father's genes

It's in my genes

It's in my mother's genes

It's just puppy fat

I will always be rejected

I will be happy when I lose weight

I will be unhappy when I lose weight

I will never be able to fix it

I will never be confident

I will never be sexy

I will never like myself

I will never like my body

I will never love my body

I will never see my body again

My weight stresses me out

My weight upsets me

Nobody wants me

They did this to me

This is because of what they did

Wherever I am I don't like it

I am always worried about what other people will think of me

I am a joke

I am controlled

I am controlled by the weight

I am defeated by the weight

I am deprived

I feel deprived

I am disgusted by my body

I am doomed to stay this way

I am embarrassed

I am embarrassing

I am fat

I am in the wrong place

I am miserable

I am never kind to myself

I am never seen or heard

I am no good

I am not good enough

I am not naturally thin

I am not responsible for my body

I am not responsible for my weight

I am of no value

I am powerless

I am secretive

I am self-destructive

I am stuck

I am too fat

I am too old to lose weight now

I believed them

I blame his/her family

I blame my DNA

I blame my family

I blame my father

I blame my grandfather

I blame my grandma

I blame my mother

I can never help myself

I can't keep the weight off

I can't look at myself

I can't put it into words

I can't succeed

I don't have time

I don't know how I feel

I don't make good decisions for my body

I don't want to be attractive

If I lose weight, I can't hide anymore

If I lose weight people won't like me

If I lose weight people will resent me

If I lose weight people will see the real me

I feel excluded

I have never been able to keep weight off

I have never been able to stay slim

I have no self-control

I have no self-discipline

I have big bones

I have lost hope

I have no control

I have no self-control

I have to accept this is the way I am

I have to count calories

I have to wear baggy horrible clothes

I need to lose weight first

I never know what to do for the best

I never look good

I resent myself

Losing weight is hard

It's all my fault

It's because I am on medication

It's the menopause

It's hereditary

It's not safe to be seen

It is too expensive to eat healthily

It is too painful to talk or think about my weight

I've tried, I've given up

I will always be fat

I won't forgive myself

I worry about it all the time

Life is a constant battle

Life is a constant struggle

My body lets me down

My weight is a constant battle

My weight keeps me safe on some level

My weight makes me disappointed

My weight makes me angry

This is because of what they said

This is who I am

Chapter 9
CORE BELIEFS: Stopping Smoking/Vaping

Clearing negative core beliefs and stuck emotions can help you to release the need for addiction and it can also help to release the fear of being without whatever that addiction is. You can also check to see which of the common negative core beliefs are linked to this issue.

It is a way to explore the reasons why you smoke and explore the life events that have contributed to your choice to smoke/vape. As with anything, if you think it may be linked to a traumatic life event then it is advisable to seek professional help and support. There are details on my website of practitioners who specialise in working with core beliefs and emotions.

You will notice that this list is much shorter than that for the Weight Management section. I would ask that even if you are trying to stop smoking you can still check through some of the core beliefs in that section. Negative core beliefs can be linked to all areas of life, and the only reason I have sectioned these off is to give you an idea of how many there are.

This list is not comprehensive, it can't be. There are thousands and thousands of negative core beliefs about all sorts of issues.

However, if any negative core beliefs come up for you outside of these lists, you will now have the tools to clear them.

If you have checked the Common Core Beliefs (page 89) and those under the heading Weight Management (page 97), you might like to have a crack at some of these. Here are some pairs of core beliefs for you to check:

I want to stop
I don't want to stop

I will not be me if I don't smoke/vape
I will be me if I don't smoke/vape

I don't believe I can stop
I do believe I can stop

I am strong
I am not strong

I am a smoker
I am a non-smoker

I don't want to be a smoker
I do want to be a smoker

I have no choice
I have a choice

I can't make my own decisions
I can make my own decisions

And here are some negative core beliefs to check out:

I need to have this habit

I will always smoke/vape

I am not me without smoking/vaping

Nobody can stop me from smoking/vaping

I love smoking/vaping

Cigarettes/vaping are my companions

Cigarettes/vaping are/is my friend

I am addicted

I always feel vulnerable

I am always bored

I am not good enough

I am not safe

I am never seen or heard

I am self-destructive

I blame my dad

I blame my family

I blame my friends

I blame my mum

I can never help myself

I can't control anything

I can't cope

I have never felt safe

I have no other option

I have to have this habit

I need to smoke/vape

It is impossible to stop

I want to hurt myself

I don't want to stop smoking/vaping

I will never be able to fix it

My life is better with smoking/vaping

Smoking/vaping calms me down

I don't like myself

I don't love myself

I am always controlled

I am always left out

I am a smoker/vaper

I am bored

I am controlled

I am in the wrong place

I am never seen or heard

I am powerless

I am scared to stop

I can't cope without smoking/vaping

I can't fix anything

I can't stop

I don't care about myself

I don't know who I will be without the smoking/vaping

I don't want to stop smoking/vaping

I enjoy smoking/vaping

I had no other choice

Smoking/vaping helps me concentrate

Smoking/vaping helps me with my stress

Smoking/vaping keeps me safe

Smoking/vaping keeps me thin

Smoking/vaping is part of who I am

Wherever I am, I don't like it

I am not in control

I do it to fit in

I will always be a smoker/vaper

I can't care for myself

I can't look after myself

I don't care for myself

I don't have a choice

Chapter 10

So...

Life happens, good stuff happens and not-so-good stuff happens. We believe stuff that is true and we believe stuff that isn't true.

To perhaps help you to mull over thinking about your life and what is true, here are a few things from my life. I'm not going to go into great detail, so these are just a series of snapshots.

Some of my life events

Drinking

At one point I was regularly doing a long 2-hour commute to work, coming home, sinking two bottles of red wine, going to bed, getting up, going to work, coming home, sinking two bottles of red wine... can you see a pattern? This went on for over 8 months until one night, when opening a third bottle, I realised what I had been doing. I had a word with myself and stopped. I still drink now but not like that and not every day! Words stopped me, I specifically talked out loud to myself. Hearing my own voice was powerful in that moment.

Wasp attack

I lawn-mowered over a wasp nest and received 30+ stings to my legs whilst on my own in our cottage in the middle of nowhere with a baby, dog, and an out-of-control lawnmower to deal with. Even so, I don't have a fear of wasps or flying things; I don't have a fear of being on my own. I have cut the grass since.

Sprinkle with...

Two marriages, two divorces, one relationship that ended after years of mental trauma. 19 job changes, 19 house moves, name changes, deaths, loss, relationships, damaging relationships, depression, birth and postnatal depression. A fear of plug holes, of being underwater, of the dark, of clowns and of balloons. Phobias, addictions, suicidal thoughts, three miscarriages and grieving over babies lost. Sleep deprivation, families together, families apart, shock, trauma, accidents and cars written off. Redundancy, court cases, isolation, weight gain and weight loss. Being homeless and being homeless with a child... the list goes on and it will continue to go on, because that is life. Using this book can hopefully help you with your past and going forward in your life with whatever life events come your way. Noticing how you react and dealing with your reaction, makes for many more happy days with only a sprinkle of the unhappy.

Moving on from life events

Just because you know how to deal with them doesn't make you exempt from life events.

What I *can* say is that knowing how to deal with emotions, knowing how to release them, dealing with all the past shite that you have hung onto, makes a life event exactly that. An event that happens, you deal with, you move on and you continue to live and love life.

> *"My research has shown me that the body can and must be healed through the mind, and the mind can and must be healed through the body."*
> Candace Pert, Ph.D.,
> *Molecules of Emotion*, page 274

What we need to do is to ensure we are giving ourselves a healthy mixture of care. So, if you have cleared emotions out of your mind, then be kind to your body, Quality Blankie Time, a lovely warm bubble bath, a massage, or something that nurtures your body.

Your emotions and negative core beliefs have been stuck and held in your mind and your body, so **Be kind to yourself.** Hug whoever you can (that you know!), swim, move your body but don't punish your body. Don't run to punish yourself, run because it brings you joy.

Ultimately, we do the best that we can do with the information and knowledge that we currently have.

So... don't beat yourself up about making the wrong choices or the wrong decisions years ago, or even recently, because you were doing the best that you could do with the information and knowledge that you had at the time.

And if you're struggling to forgive people and want to stay angry at them, consider that they were doing the best that they could do with the information and knowledge that *they* had, and who knows what old shite they had been told.

So...

Life happens...

How you react to life....

Well, my lovelies, that is up to you!

I know you can do it...

You need to know that you can do it too.

So... give it a whirl, try it, say some words, and see if they get rid of stuff. I have been doing it for years and I definitely will be carrying on doing it too.

It is so easy when you know how 😊 and now everyone else has done their bit in science, we can now do our bit at this time. Let's carry it forward so that self-care is just a normal part of life.

Oh, and in case nobody told you... You can do it, YOU are amazing... put that in your core belief pipe and smoke it!! xx

APPENDIX

Practitioners

Amanda Peet founded EDT (Emotional Dowsing Techniques) and trains other practitioners on how to use EDT with their clients in their current practice.

To clients: If you wanted to have a one-to-one related to a specific issue, the practitioners listed via the link below will use the same techniques used in this book, with one key difference. Instead of you reading through lists of core beliefs, the practitioner will use dowsing to elicit a YES/NO answer. This works in a similar way to muscle testing and through this they will pinpoint specific negative core beliefs that will help you with any issues.

You don't need to put any life experiences into words – you just need to state the emotions that you are feeling. Likewise, if you struggle to identify how you are feeling, they can help you to unpick that too.

To practitioners: If you would like to add EDT to your practice, please apply via the site below. The EDT Practitioner courses are fully accredited with the CMA.

For more information and a full list, please visit:

www.amandapeet.org.uk/practitioners

"I absolutely love working with Amanda and EDT. I'm getting fabulous results with clients using EDT since training with Amanda to be a Practitioner. I run a coaching business and it's the perfect complement to other modalities that I use. Aside from clearing lots of emotions, we've also cleared money and success blocks where my clients have signed up new clients themselves and brought in money and new opportunities within a day or two of doing the work with me.

I love that you can blend EDT with what you already use. The course itself is great, but Amanda also offers amazing aftercare too so that you feel fully supported in your ongoing work. I live in Scotland and couldn't make the journey to the training in Devon, so I attended the training virtually. It was as if I was there with everyone, loved it! If you want to help your clients, and like a bit of woo, then sign up. You won't regret it!"

Ruby McGuire, Business Coach and Mentor

Shortcuts

If you use muscle testing or dowsing, you can use these skills to shortcut the lists in this book and muscle test or dowse your way around them to see what is true for you.

If you want to learn how to dowse, you might be interested in:

The Dowsing Programme

 Amanda has developed an online course that you can enjoy from the comfort of your own home with your blankie.

This shows you how to dowse, how to dowse a list (shortcut), clear emotions, clear negative core beliefs, check what your system currently needs in terms of food, water, sleep and exercise, as well as many other ways you can use dowsing today in a highly technological world.

The Dowsing Programme includes:

- 8 Masterclass videos to watch at your own pace (no time limit)
- 7 resource sheets to download
- Access to a closed Facebook group to become part of our dowsing community, which is an excellent place to share

progress. Bonus resource sheets, updates and links to additional free resources are posted in this group too.

- If you don't like Facebook, you can receive updates via email instead, so you still obtain our comprehensive aftercare and support.

For more info, please visit
www.amandapeet.org.uk/level-1-online

How has core belief work helped others? Some comments from those that are using the Programme:

"Doing core belief work as part of my self-care I am now more confident with a fear I had – getting on and off trains. Plus released baggage I'd been carrying around for years. Doing core belief work as part of my self-care has made me more confident in the things I feared."

Carol Clark

"By doing core belief work regularly it has been possible to help myself and others to become happier and more healthy in many aspects of living.

I see it as having a spring clean of stuck beliefs of self that hold us back and cause us pain.

Pressing a reset button that's sets us free!

Thank you Amanda, the programme you have developed is life changing. xxx"

Debbie Bales

"Doing core belief work as part of my self-care has helped me to identify issues, that may have been holding me back from fulfilling my full potential. I am now equipped to recognise core beliefs and any emotions attached to them, releasing them using the words that Amanda has taught me; in doing so I can continue to grow and flourish. Doing core belief work as part of my self-care has helped me like nothing else has or could."

Sadie Martinez

By doing core belief work regularly I have been able to recover from anorexia and can finally love myself and feel confident exactly as I am.

Kim Marshall

Acknowledgements

Team Sam Pearce at SWATT Books, thank you so much for your amazing and professional help throughout my first self-publishing journey. Mark, you have completely polished my book to make it more shiny. Thank you.

I have some special friends who have supported me through my life and, in some cases, have helped me to survive. They have never said: get a proper job. They have never said: do something else. They have supported me fully and completely without wanting to change me, even those who don't really understand what I do . For those friends I am truly grateful. Some have also been my guinea pigs: you know who you are!

So, a big massive lovely thank you to Mum (yes, she is my friend too), my (unofficial) stepdad Frank, my Dad and, in alphabetical order because I can't decide how else to list you lovelies: to Dani Blant, Libby Brennan, Mr and Mrs Borrows, Jo Cooke, Dawn Goodfellow, Hannah Hale, Wendy Harrower, Bex Hill, Sylvia Jackson, Oliver Jenkin, Yvonne Johnson, Victoria (Johnson) but always Lax to me, Ruby Jones, Eileen Kelly, Ruby McGuire, Kathy Morgan, The Shawleys (all of you xx), Neil and Charlotte Simpson, Anna Wilkinson, Hilary Wilkinson, and to the mums on the school run (sometimes the only adults I see during the week). To my EDT Practitioners who help clients daily . Hugs and kisses. I love you all xx

To all the family (including all the aunties, uncles and cousins... loads of 'em!) and friends that I know, my special people, thank you for being kind and caring. I love you _____: you can write your name here because you have all been a part of my life in one way or another.

To all those people who have been mean and horrid to me, thank you to you too. Because I have dealt with my reaction to your words and actions, I have been able to deep clean my brain and really get rid of all the crap. So, thank you for being my sh*t shifters.

And thank you to you... yes you, reading this... the Shiny Happy People. Thank you for reading my book. Now go, be off with ya, clear out what you no longer need and what is holding you back.

With love

Amanda xx

The How

1. Look at the list of emotions/negative core beliefs.

2. Either start at the top of the list or see which ones jump out at you from the page.

3. Say that emotion/negative core belief out loud.

4. Don't race ahead, one at a time.

5. Feel how that emotion/negative core belief feels when you say "My system is holding onto… *[state emotion/negative core belief]*" Does that feel true, false, or somewhere in-between for you?

6. If true or somewhere in-between, go to step 7. If false, then go to Step 1 to find the next emotion or negative core belief and repeat the process.

7. Say **The Words** out loud for releasing emotions/negative core beliefs. **The Words** are below.

8. Take a deep breath.

9. If any other emotions came to mind whilst you were saying the words, write them down and do ***The Words*** for each of those too.

10. Go back to your original emotion/negative core belief and say, "My system is holding onto… *[state emotion/negative core belief]*" See how that feels, true, false, or somewhere in-between.

11. If true or somewhere in-between, go to step 7. If false, then go to Step 1 to find the next emotion or negative core belief and repeat the process.

At this point, if you have cleared a few emotions/negative core beliefs, you might need a bit of Quality Blankie Time.

The Words

EMOTIONS – THE WORDS

Say these words out loud:

Even though I feel… *[state the emotion]*

I am asking my subconscious to release this now.

I am asking my subconscious to release what needs to be released, and change what needs to change, so my conscious mind doesn't have to.

That was then, this is now.

That emotion of… *[state emotion]* is no longer working for me.

Releasing… *[state emotion]* safely and completely, through all space and time and throughout my whole system.

Now you have completed that section, take a deep breath, give yourself a few minutes before checking back with yourself, or moving onto the next one.

Say the emotion out loud again and feel its intensity. If you can still feel it, say the words again or have a look at the list. There might be something else linked to it.

Always good to drink water whilst doing this.

CORE BELIEFS – THE WORDS

Say these words out loud:

Even though I have this core belief... *[state core belief]*

I am now choosing to release this.

I am asking my subconscious to release this now.

I am asking my subconscious to release what needs to release, and change what needs to change, so my conscious mind doesn't have to.

That was then, this is now.

That core belief of... *[state core belief]* is no longer working for me.

Releasing... *[state core belief]* safely and completely, through all space and time and throughout my whole system.

Now you have completed that section, take a deep breath, give yourself a few minutes before checking back with yourself, and if any memories or flashbacks came up, write down what they are and then tackle them one at a time.

If you don't release any emotions which conjure up any more memories or flashbacks, then that's fine. I very rarely get flashbacks; I trust that my superfast subconscious is dealing with it.

Say the negative core belief out loud again and feel if it is true, false, or somewhere in-between. It is normal for some people to not know what they think about that statement. If that is the case, sleep on it and say it again out loud the following day after you have woken up. How does it feel then?

Always good to drink water whilst doing this.

CORE BELIEF BALANCE – THE WORDS

Say these words out loud:

> Even though I have these core beliefs... *[state the pair of core beliefs, e.g. I can, I can't]*

> I am now choosing to release these.

> I am asking my subconscious to unravel this now.

> I am asking my subconscious to release what needs to release, and change what needs to change, so my conscious mind doesn't have to.

> That was then, this is now.

> I am asking for those core beliefs of... *[state the pair of core beliefs]* to be brought back into a healthy balance.

> Releasing what is not working for me safely and completely, through all space and time, and throughout my whole system.

Printed in Great Britain
by Amazon

16974678R00072